On Duties

On Duties

(De Officiis)

Marcus Tullius Cicero

Translated with an Introduction and Notes by Andrew P. Peabody

WAKING LION PRESS

ISBN 978-1-43411-727-4

Published by Waking Lion Press, an imprint of The Editorium

The Editorium, LLC
West Valley City, UT 84128-3917
wakinglionpress.com
wakinglion@editorium.com

Contents

Introduction

There are two systems of ethical philosophy, which in every age divide speculative moralists, and are recognized with a more or less distinct consciousness in the conduct of life by all in whom the moral sense has attained mature development. They are, indeed, in different ages and by different writers stated more or less explicitly, in widely varying terminology, and with modifications from culture, religion, national character, and individual proclivities. They are, also, sometimes blended by an eclecticism which cannot wholly transcend the lower, yet feels the intense attraction of the higher sphere. One system is that which makes virtue a means; the other, that which makes it an end. According to the one, we are to practise virtue for the good that will come of it to ourselves or our fellow-beings; according to the other, we are to practise virtue for its own sake, for its intrinsic fitness and excellence, without reference to ulterior consequences, save when, and so far as, those consequences are essential factors in determining the intrinsic quality of the action.

Of course, this general division admits of obvious subdivisions. The former system includes the selfish and the utilitarian theory of morals,— the selfish making the pursuit of our own happiness our duty, and adaptation to that end the sole standard of right; the utilitarian identifying virtue with benevolence, accounting the greatest good of the greatest number the supreme aim, and beneficent utility the ultimate standard of duty. The alternative system, according to which virtue is to be practised, not for what it does, but for what it is, includes, also, various definitions of virtue, according as its standard is deemed to be intrinsic fitness, accordance with the aesthetic nature, the verdict of the moral sense, or conformity to the will of God. These latter theories, widely as they differ, agree in representing the right as having a validity independent of circumstances and of human judgment, as unaffected by the time-and-place element, as possessed of characteristics connate, indelible, eternal; while the selfish and utilitarian schools alike represent it as mutable, dependent on circumstances, varying with time and place, and possessed of no attributes distinctively its own.

In Cicero's time the left and the right wing in ethical philosophy were represented by the Epicureans and the Stoics respectively, while the Peripatetics held a middle ground. The Epicureans regarded happiness—or, according to their founder, painlessness—as the sole aim and end of moral conduct, and thus resolved all virtue into prudence, or judicious self-love,—a doctrine which with such a disciple as Pliny the Younger identified virtue with the highest self-culture as alone conducive to the happiness of the entire selfhood, intellectual and spiritual as well as bodily; but with Horace and his like, and with Rousseau, who professed adherence to that school, afforded license and amnesty to the most debasing sensuality.

The Stoics regarded virtue as the sole aim and end of life, and virtue is, in their philosophy, the conformity of the will and conduct to universal nature,—intrinsic fitness thus being the law and the criterion of the right. Complete conformity, or perfect virtue, is, according to this school, attainable only by the truly wise; and its earlier disciples, while by no means certain that this ideal perfectness had ever been realized in human form even by Zeno, the great master, yet admitted no moral distinction between those who fell but little short of perfection and those who had made no progress toward it. The later Stoics, however, recognized degrees of goodness, and were diligent expositors and teachers of the duties within the scope of those not truly wise, by the practice of which there might be an ever nearer approach to perfection. This philosophy was, from Cicero's time till Christianity gained ascendency, the only antiseptic that preserved Roman society from utter and remediless corruption.

The Peripatetic philosophy makes virtue to consist in moderation, or the avoidance of extremes, and places each of the individual virtues midway between opposite vices, as temperance between excess and asceticism; generosity between prodigality and avarice; meekness between irascibility and pusillanimity. It admits the reality of the intrinsically right as distinguished from the merely expedient or useful; but it maintains that happiness is the supreme object and end of life, and that for this end, virtue, though essential, is not sufficient without external goods,—so that the wisely virtuous man, while he will never violate the right, will pursue by all legitimate means such outward advantages as may be within his reach.

The New Academy, whose philosophy was a blending of Platonism and Pyrrhonism, while it denied the attainableness of objective truth, maintained that on all subjects of speculative philosophy probability is attainable, and that wherever there is scope for action, the moral agent is bound to act in accordance with probability,—of two courses to pursue that for which the more and the better reasons can be given. The disciples of this school accepted provisionally the Peripatetic ethics.

Cicero professed to belong to the New Academy, and its ethical position was in close accordance with his nature. Opinion rather than belief was his mental habit,—strong opinion, indeed, yet less than certainty. His instincts as an advocate—often induced by professional exigencies, not only to cast doubt on what he had previously affirmed, but with the ardor of one who threw himself with his whole soul into the case in hand to feel such doubt before he gave it utterance—made the scepticism of this school congenial to him. At the same time, his love of elegant ease and luxury and his lack of moral enterprise— though not of courage when emergencies were forced upon him—were in closer affinity with the practical ethics of the Peripatetics than with the more rigid system of the Stoics; while his pure moral taste and his genuine reverence for the right brought him into sympathy with the Stoic school. Under no culture short of that Christian regeneration which is less a culture than a power could he have become heroically virtuous; under no conceivable influence could he, such as he was in his early manhood, have become grossly vicious. He believed in virtue, admired it, loved it. His aesthetic nature was pre-eminently true and pure. His private character indicates high-toned principle. In an age when all things were venal, no charge of corruption was ever urged against him, even by an enemy. He neither bought office, nor sold its functions. Associating familiarly with well-known convivialists, who regarded a wine-debauch as always a welcome episode in the pursuits whether of war or of peace, we have no vestige of a proof that he ever transgressed the bounds of temperance, and there is not a word in his writings that indicates any sympathy with excesses of the table. Living at a time when licentiousness in its foulest forms was professed without shame and practised without rebuke, we have reason to believe that he led a chaste life from his youth; and though as an advocate he was sometimes obliged to refer to subjects and transactions offensive to purity, and in his letters there are passages which might seem out of place in the correspondence of a Christian scholar of the nineteenth century, it may be doubted whether in all his extant writings there is a single sentence inconsistent with what a purist of his own age would have deemed a blameless moral character.

He has been, indeed, charged by some of his biographers with motives of the lowest order in the divorce of the mother of his children after a union of thirty years, and his marriage with a young heiress, his own ward. But by the best standard that he knew, though not by the Christian standard so profligately ignored and outraged in our own section of Christendom, he was more than justified. His wife was no little of a virago, had wasted a great deal of money for him in his absence, and had willed property under her control in such a way as to give him just displeasure; and it appears from his letters that he exercised the then unquestioned right of divorce solely on these grounds, with no specific marriage in view, and that the alliance which he actually made was preceded by overtures both to and from other candidates for that honor. Moreover, the charge of mercenary views in this marriage is negatived by its speedy dissolution on his part, with the sacrifice of the entire and large fortune which it brought to him, on the sole ground that his bride had manifested unseemly satisfaction in the death of his daughter Tullia, whom she regarded as her rival in her husband's affection.

Yet there were heights of virtue beyond Cicero's scope. He was wholly destitute of the martyr-spirit. He was much of a Sybarite in his habits. His many villas, furnished with equal taste and splendor, gave him the sumptuous surroundings and the aesthetic leisure without which he could not regard even virtue as sufficient for his happiness, and times of enforced absence from wonted pursuits and enjoyments were filled with unmanly complaint and self-commiseration. He loved applause, suffered keenly from unpopularity, and vacillated in his political allegiance, sometimes with the breeze of public opinion, sometimes with his faith in the fortunes of an eminent leader. He often worshipped with manifest sincerity the ascending star, and had little sympathy with fallen greatness. He was thoroughly patriotic, would have sacrificed for his country anything and everything except his own fame, and coveted nothing so much as opportunities like that afforded by the Catilinian conspiracy for winning celebrity by signal service to the republic. He had, too, large and profound wisdom as a statesman; but his best judgment generally came too late for action, so that had he derived a surname from classic fable, it would have been Epimetheus, not Prometheus. As an advocate he was supple and many-sided, yet he always impresses his reader with his sincerity, and probably a prime element of his pre-eminent success in the courts was the capacity of making a cause his own, and throwing into it for the time genuine feeling and not its mere eloquent semblance.

His lot was cast in an age when only an iron will could have maintained, along with the conscious integrity which, as I think, characterized Cicero's whole life, the perfect self-consistency which no stress could bend or warp. When we compare him with his most illustrious contemporaries, it is impossible not to assign to him a preeminent place both as to private virtues and as to public services. It is only when we try him by his own standard that we have a vivid sense of his deficiencies and shortcomings.

Cicero's only son, with the heritage of his name, Marcus Tullius, seems to have inherited few of his father's distinguishing characteristics, and not improbably may have borne, in some respects, a close moral kindred to his high-spirited mother. He was impetuous, irascible, headstrong, brave as a soldier, and though indolent except when roused to action, not without ability and learning. At the age of sixteen he served with great credit in Pompey's army. After the defeat of Pharsalia he was sent to Athens to complete his education. He fell there into habits of gross dissipation, being led astray by one of his teachers. He, however, yielded to his father's earnest remonstrances, expressed great grief and shame for his misconduct, and entered upon a regular and studious course of life, winning high credit with Cratippus his teacher, and receiving warm commendation from his father's friends resident or sojourning in Athens. He subsequently fought with distinction under Marcus Brutus, and after the battle of Philippi joined Sextus Pompeius in Sicily. Returning to Rome when peace was concluded with the Triumvirate, he was an object of special regard with Augustus, and after holding several offices of lower grade, became his colleague in the consulship. He afterward went as proconsul to Asia Minor, where his name drops from history, which but for his father might never have found place for it.

When it appeared that Brutus and Cassius had effected nothing for the republic, and Antony was becoming all-powerful in the state, in the spring of 44 b. c., Cicero, deeming his life insecure, left Rome, and spent the summer successively at several of his villas in Western Italy. He beguiled his disappointment and sorrow at the issue of public affairs by philosophy and ethics, and this summer seems to have been, at least for posterity, the most fruitful season of his life, being the epoch of the completion of his *Tusculan Disputations* and his *De Natura Deorum*, and of the composition of several of his smaller treatises. In June of that year he says, in a letter to Atticus, that he is writing for his son's benefit an elaborate treatise on Morals. "On what subject," he asks, "can a father better write to a son?" In the latter part of the summer he started on a journey to Athens to visit his son, but was recalled by the intelligence of a probable understanding on amicable terms between Antony and the Senate. Deceived in this hope, he repaired to Rome, and pronounced his first Philippic against Antony in the beginning of September. In November he writes again about his ethical work, tells Atticus that he has completed two books and is busy on the third, and announces and explains the title. The work was completed before the end of the year.

Cicero's time was a period of eclecticism in philosophy, especially so among the cultivated Romans, with whom philosophy was not indigenous, but a comparatively recent importation. Cicero himself was pre-eminently a lover of philosophical thought, study, and discussion, and probably was more intimately conversant with the history of opinions and the contents of books in that department than any man of his time; yet he seems to have lacked profound convictions on the subjects at issue among the several schools. Thus in the *De Officiis*, while he repeatedly professes his adherence to the New Academy and the Peripatetic doctrine of morals, he bases his discussion on the Stoic theory, and intimates very clearly that he thought his son safer under the rigid discipline of the Stoic school than under the more lax though wise tuition of his Peripatetic preceptor. It is as if a Mohammedan, while recognizing the divine mission of the Arab prophet, were to write for his son a treatise on the ethics of the New Testament as better adapted than the moral system of the Koran for the training and confirming of a young man in the practice of virtue.

This treatise, then, may be regarded as an exposition of the ethical system of the Stoics of Cicero's time, yet with a special limitation, purpose, and adaptation. It is not designed for the ideally perfect philosopher, nor for a candidate for that exalted position, but for one on the lower plane of common life. It therefore defines not the moral consciousness of the truly wise man, but the specific duties by the practice of which one may grow into the semblance of true wisdom. Nor does it purport to be a compendium even of these duties. It is simply a directory for a young Roman of high rank and promise, who is going to enter upon public life, and to be a candidate for office and honor in the state. It prescribes the self-training, the social relations, and the habits of living, by which such a youth may both deserve and attain distinction and eminence, and the respect and confidence of his fellow-citizens. Of course, many of the details in this treatise were of merely local and transient import and value; but its underlying principles are in such close harmony with the absolute and eternal right that they can never become obsolete. At the same time, the division and arrangement of the treatise give it, so far as I know, the precedence over all other ethical treatises ancient or modern. The division is exhaustive. The arrangement is such as to leave an open space for the insertion and full treatment of any topic within the scope of ethical philosophy.

The First Book treats of the Right. The right consists in accordance with nature, with the nature of things, with the nature of man. Hence is derived its imperative obligation upon the human conscience. Its duties are evolved from man's own consciousness. Man by his very nature desires knowledge, and craves materials for the active exercise of his cognitive powers. He is by his birth, by his instinctive cravings, by the necessity of his daily life, a gregarious being, a member of a family, of society, of the state, and as such cannot but recognize justice, including benevolence, as his imperative duty. He postulates distinction, eminence, a position from which he can look down on earthly fortunes as beneath him, and can sacrifice all exterior good for the service of mankind and the attainment of merited fame. He has also an innate sense of order, proportion, harmony, which can satisfy itself only by practical reference to the due time, place, manner, and measure of whatever is done or said. Hence the four virtues of Prudence or Wisdom, Justice, Fortitude or Magnanimity, and Order, Temperance, or Moderation. These virtues in their broadest significance include all human obligations, and form a series of divisions, under one or another of which may be classed every specific duty. Under each of these heads Cicero shows what was demanded by the highest sentiment of his time from a youth of spotless fame and of honorable ambition.

The Second Book has Expediency, or Utility, for its subject. Outside of the province of duty or of things required there is large room for choice among things permitted,—consistent with the Right, yet forming no part of it. The question that underlies this Book is, By what honorable methods, other than the discharge of express duty, can a young man secure for himself the favor, gratitude, assistance, and—in case of need—the suffrages of his fellow-citizens? This Book has its proper place in a treatise on morals, because it is the author's aim throughout to discriminate between the immoral and the legitimate modes of obtaining reputation and popularity.

The Third Book deals with the alleged or seeming discrepancy between the Expedient and the Right. Cicero denies the possibility of such mutual repugnance, and maintains that whatever is expedient must of necessity be right, and that what is right cannot be otherwise than expedient.

In this translation I have attempted to give, not a word-for-word version of the Latin text, but a literal transcript in English of what I suppose that Cicero meant to write in his own tongue. I have not used his moods and tenses in the instances in which our English idiom would employ a different form of the verb. I have not infrequently omitted the connective and illative words that bind sentence to sentence, in cases in which we should use no such words.[1] In the few obscure passages I have sought the aid of the best commentators, but have generally found them hazy or ambiguous in their interpretation where there was any room for doubt. I may have made mistakes in translating; but if so, it has not been for lack of close and careful study, with the help of the best editions which I could procure for myself or find in the Harvard College Library.

I have used Beier's text as the basis for my translation, and have preferred not to deviate from it even where a different reading seemed to me intrinsically probable; for in every such instance Beier gives satisfactory reasons for his preferred reading, and destitute as I am of the needed apparatus for textual criticism, I cannot but regard his judgment in such a case as much better than my own.

---

1. I am strongly impressed with the belief that such words were largely employed as catch-words for the eye, and that they served the purpose now effected by punctuation and by the capital letters at the beginning of sentences. This opinion cannot of course be verified; yet could we have phonographic reports of Cicero's orations, I am inclined to think that we should miss some of the conjunctions that are found in their written form. As to Greek particles I have no right to an opinion; but I will hazard the conjecture that they would have been scattered with a more sparing hand, had the art of punctuation been coeval with "the letters Cadmus gave."

Book I

1. Although you, my son Marcus, having listened for a year to Cratippus, and that at Athens, ought to be well versed in the maxims and principles of philosophy, on account of the paramount authority both of the teacher and of the city,—the former being able to enrich you with knowledge; the latter, with examples,—yet, as for my own benefit I have always connected Latin with Greek, and have done so, not only in philosophy, but also in my self-training as a public speaker, I think that you, too, ought to do the same, in order that you may be equally capable of either style of discourse.[1] To this end I have, as it seems to me, been of no small service to my fellow-citizens, so that not only those ignorant of Greek literature, but highly educated men also, think that they have gained somewhat from me, both as to public speaking and as to philosophical discussion. Therefore, while you will be the pupil of the first philosopher of our time, and will continue so as long as you please,—and that ought to be as long as you can profit by his instruction,—yet by reading my writings, which dissent very little from the Peripatetics (for both they and I regard ourselves as disciples both of Socrates and of Plato), though on the subjects of discussion I would have you freely exercise your own judgment, you will certainly acquire a fuller command of the Latin tongue. Nor in speaking thus ought I to be regarded as presumptuous. For while in the science of philosophy I may have many superiors, if I claim for myself what belongs properly to the orator, aptness, perspicuity, and elegance of diction, since I have passed my life in this pursuit, it is not without a good measure of right that I proffer the claim. Wherefore I earnestly exhort you, my Cicero, to read carefully not only my orations, but these books of mine on philosophy, which already in bulk are nearly equal to the orations.

---

1. Either philosophical discussion or oratory.

For while in oratory there is a greater force of expression, the more even and moderate style of writing that belongs to philosophy ought also to be cultivated. And indeed I do not see that it has fallen to any Greek author to exercise himself in both styles, and to pursue at once forensic eloquence and unimpassioned philosophical discussion; unless, perchance, this may be said of Demetrius Phalereus,[1]—a keen disputant, and at the same time an orator, though of no great power, yet with a winning grace by which one might recognize him as a disciple of Theophrastus. But what proficiency I have made in either style let others judge; I certainly have pursued both. Indeed, I think that Plato, too, if he had been disposed to attempt forensic eloquence, would have spoken with equal fluency and power; and that Demosthenes, if he had retained and had wished to put into writing what he had learned from Plato, would have done so in a style both graceful and magnificent. I have the same opinion of Aristotle and Isocrates, each of whom, charmed with his own department, held the other in low esteem.

2. But, having determined to write expressly for your benefit something at the present time, much hereafter, I have thought it best to begin with what is most suitable both to your age and to my parental authority. Now, among the many important and useful subjects in philosophy that have been discussed by philosophers with precision and fulness of statement, their traditions and precepts concerning the duties of life seem to have the widest scope. Indeed, no part of life, whether in public or in private affairs, abroad or at home, in your personal conduct or your social relations, can be free from the claims of duty; and it is in the observance of duty that lies all the honor of life, in its neglect, all the shame. This, too, is a theme common to all philosophers. For who would dare to call himself a philosopher, if he took no cognizance of duty? Yet there are some schools of philosophy that utterly pervert duty by the view which they propose as to the supreme good, and as to the opposite extreme of evil. For he who so interprets the supreme good as to disjoin it from virtue, and measures it by his own convenience, and not by the standard of right,—he, I say, if he be consistent with himself, and be not sometimes overcome by natural goodness, can cultivate

---

1. He was known chiefly as an orator; but the list of his numerous works comprises philosophy, history, and poetry. Driven from Athens, he took refuge in Alexandria; and it was owing to his influence that Ptolemy Lagi commenced the collection of books which grew into the famous Alexandrian library. No probably genuine work of Demetrius Phalereus is now extant.

neither friendship, nor justice, nor generosity; nor can he possibly be brave while he esteems pain as the greatest of evils, or temperate while he regards pleasure as the supreme good. These things, though too obvious to need discussion, I yet have discussed elsewhere. Those schools, therefore, can, if self-consistent, say nothing about duty; nor can any precepts of duty, decisive, immutable, in accordance with nature, be promulgated, except by those who maintain that the right is to be sought solely,[1] or chiefly,[2] for its own sake. This prerogative belongs to the Stoics, the Academics, and the Peripatetics; for the opinions of Ariston, Pyrrho, and Herillus[3] were long since exploded, though they might fittingly have discussed subjects pertaining to duty, if they had left any ground for the preference of one thing over another, so that there might be a way open for the ascertainment of duty. In this treatise I shall follow the Stoics, not as a translator, but drawing from their fountains at my own discretion and judgment, as much, and in such way, as may seem good.

I think it fit, however, since duty is to be my sole subject, to define duty at the outset.[4] I am surprised that Panaetius should not have done this; for the rational treatment of any subject ought to take its start from definition, that readers may understand what the author is writing about.

3. The discussion of duty is twofold. One division relates to the supreme good in itself considered; the other, to the rules by which the conduct of life may in all its parts be brought into conformity with the supreme good. Under the first head belong such questions as these: Whether all duties are of perfect obligation; whether any one duty is

---

1. As was the case with the Stoics.

2. As was the case with the Peripatetics, and, hypothetically, with the Academics.

3. Ariston, while he regarded virtue as the supreme good, maintained that among the external conditions and objects with which duty is conversant, there is no ground for preference, therefore no reason why one should be sought or pursued rather than another. Pyrrho, the founder of the school of the Sceptics, in denying the possibility of attaining any objective truth, denied the possibility of determining any condition, object, or action to be better than any other. Herillus—like Ariston, a professed Stoic—regarded knowledge as the supreme good, and external life, with all its doings and objects, though practically necessary, as of no ethical value, because not contributing to the supreme good.

4. Yet Cicero leaves duty (*officium*) undefined. *Officium* may be abbreviated from *opificium*, i.e., work-doing; or it may be derived from *ob* and *facio*, in which case it denotes doing on account of, or for a reason, and would include all acts for which a reason, i.e., a right reason, can be given. I am inclined to think that it is in this latter sense that Cicero made choice and use of the word.

greater than another; and, in general, inquiries of a similar kind. But the duties for which rules are laid down belong, indeed, to the supreme good, as means to an end; yet this is the less obvious, because they seem rather to have reference to the ordering of common life. It is of these that I am going to treat in the present work. There is also another division of duty. Duty may be said to be either contingent or perfect. We may, I think, give the name of perfect duty to the absolute right, which the Greeks term χατόρθωμα·[1] while contingent duty is what they call χαθηχον.[2] According to their definitions, what is right in itself is perfect duty; that for the doing of which a satisfactory reason can be given is a contingent duty.

According to Panaetius, in determining what we ought to do there are three questions to be considered. It is first to be determined whether the contemplated act is right or wrong,—a matter as to which there often are opposite opinions. Then there is room for inquiry or consultation whether the act under discussion is conducive to convenience and pleasure, to affluence and free command of outward goods, to wealth, to power, in fine, to the means by which one can benefit himself and those dependent on him; and here the question turns on expediency. The third class of cases is when what appears to be expedient seems repugnant to the right. For when expediency lays, as it were, violent hands upon us, and the right seems to recall us to itself, the mind is distracted, and laden with two-fold anxiety as to the course of action. In this distribution of the subject, while a division ought by all means to be exhaustive, there are two omissions. Not only is the question of right or wrong as to an act wont to be considered, but also the question, of two right things which is the more right; equally, of two expedient things which is the more expedient. Thus we see that the division which Panaetius thought should be threefold ought to be distributed under five heads. First, then, I am to treat of the right, but under two heads; then, in the same way, of the expedient; lastly, of their seeming conflict.

4. In the beginning, animals of every species were endowed with the instinct that prompts them to take care of themselves as to life and bodily well-being, to shun whatever threatens to do them harm, and to seek and provide whatever is necessary for subsistence, as food, shelter, and other things of this sort. The appetite for sexual union for

---

1. The *direct*, i.e., the intrinsically right.
2. The *fitting*, i.e., that which is rendered right by circumstances.

the production of offspring is, also, common to all animals, together with a certain degree of care for their offspring.

But between man and beast there is this essential difference, that the latter, moved by sense alone, adapts himself only to that which is present in place and time, having very little cognizance of the past or the future. Man, on the other hand—because he is possessed of reason, by which he discerns consequences, sees the causes of things, understands the rise and progress of events, compares similar objects, and connects and associates the future with the present—easily takes into view the whole course of life, and provides things necessary for it. Nature too, by virtue of reason, brings man into relations of mutual intercourse and society with his fellow-men; generates in him a special love for his children; prompts him to promote and attend social gatherings and public assemblies; and awakens in him the desire to provide what may suffice for the support and nourishment, not of himself alone, but of his wife, his children, and others whom he holds dear and is bound to protect. This care rouses men's minds, and makes them more efficient in action. The research and investigation of truth, also, are a special property of man. Thus, when we are free from necessary occupations, we want to see, or hear, or learn something, and regard the knowledge of things either secret or wonderful as essential to our living happily and well.[1] To this desire for seeing the truth is annexed a certain craving for precedence, insomuch that the man well endowed by nature is willing to render obedience to no one, unless to a preceptor, or a teacher, or one who holds a just and legitimate sway for the general good. Hence are derived greatness of mind and contempt for the vicissitudes of human fortune. Nor does it indicate any feeble force of nature and of reason, that of all animals man alone has a sense of order, and decency, and moderation in action and in speech. Thus no other animal feels the beauty, elegance, symmetry, of the things that he sees; while by nature and reason, man, transferring these qualities from the eyes to the mind, considers that much more, even, are beauty, consistency, and order to be preserved in purposes and acts, and takes heed that he do nothing indecorous or effeminate, and still more, that in all his thoughts and deeds he neither do nor

---

1. It will be seen that, in the sequel, Cicero transposes the virtues springing from man's social nature and his desire for knowledge, placing wisdom or prudence first, and assigning the second place to justice.

think anything lascivious. From these elements the right, which is the object of our inquiry, is composed and created; and this, even if it be not ennobled in title, yet is honorable, and even if no one praise it, we truly pronounce it in its very nature worthy of all praise.

5. You behold, indeed, my son Marcus, the very form and, as it were, the countenance of the right, which, were it seen by the eyes, as Plato says, would awaken the intensest love of wisdom. But whatever is right springs from one of four sources. It consists either in the perception and skilful treatment of the truth; or in maintaining good-fellowship with men, giving to every one his due, and keeping faith in contracts and promises; or in the greatness and strength of a lofty and unconquered mind; or in the order and measure that constitute moderation and temperance.[1] Although these four are connected and intertwined with one another, yet duties of certain kinds proceed from each of them; as from the division first named, including wisdom and prudence, proceed the investigation and discovery of truth, as the peculiar office of that virtue. For in proportion as one sees clearly what is the inmost and essential truth with regard to any subject, and can demonstrate it with equal acuteness and promptness, he is wont to be regarded, and justly, as of transcendent discretion and wisdom. Therefore truth is submitted to this virtue as the material of which it treats, and with which it is conversant. The other three virtues have for their sphere the providing and preserving of those things on which the conduct of life depends, so that the fellowship and union of society may be maintained, and that superiority and greatness of mind may shine forth, not only in the increase of resources and the acquisition of objects of desire for one's self, and for those dependent on him, but much more in a position from which one can look down on these very things. But order, and consistency, and moderation, and similar qualities have their scope in affairs that demand not merely the movement of the mind, but some outward action; for it is by bringing to the concerns of daily life a certain method and order that we shall maintain honor and propriety.

---

1. These four virtues may be easily so enlarged in their scope as to cover the whole of life, and to comprehend the entire duty of man. Thus, Prudence embraces all selfward obligations; Justice (which includes benevolence, and is not exclusive of piety), all duties to fellow-beings; Fortitude (including patience, submission, and courage), duty with reference to objects and events beyond one's control; Order (in time, place, and measure), duty with reference to objects under one's control.

6. Of the four heads into which I have divided the nature and force of the right, the first, which consists in the cognizance of truth, bears the closest relation to human nature. For we are all attracted and drawn to the desire of knowledge and wisdom, in which we deem it admirable to excel, but both an evil and a shame to fail, to be mistaken, to be ignorant, to be deceived. In this quest of knowledge, both natural and right, there are two faults to be shunned,—one, the taking of unknown things for known, and giving our assent to them too hastily, which fault he who wishes to escape (and all ought so to wish) will give time and diligence to reflect on the subjects proposed for his consideration. The other fault is that some bestow too great zeal and too much labor on things obscure and difficult, and at the same time useless. These faults being shunned, whatever labor and care may be bestowed on subjects becoming a virtuous mind and worth knowing, will be justly commended. Thus we learn that Caius Sulpicius was versed in astronomy,[1] as I myself knew Sextius Pompeius to be in geometry,[2] as many are in logic, many in civil law,—all which sciences are concerned in the investigation of truth, but by whose pursuit duty will not suffer one to be drawn away from the active management of affairs. For the reputation of virtue consists wholly in active life, from which, however, there is often a respite, and frequent opportunities are afforded for returning to the pursuit of knowledge. At the same time mental activity, which never ceases, may retain us, without conscious effort, in meditation on the subjects of our study. But all thought and mental action ought to be occupied either in taking counsel as to the things that are right and that appertain to a good and happy life, or in the pursuit of wisdom and knowledge. I have thus spoken of the first source of duty.

7. Of the remaining three heads, the principle which constitutes the bond of human society and of a virtual community of life has the widest scope. Of this there are two divisions,—justice, in which consists the greatest lustre of virtue, and which those who possess are termed

---

1. When serving in the Macedonian war, as military tribune under Aemilius Paulus, he predicted an eclipse of the moon, and obtained liberty to announce his prediction to the assembled army, thus precluding the else inevitable terror and foreboding which pervaded the Macedonian army, and very probably turning the scale in favor of the Romans in the then imminent battle in which Perseus, the Macedonian king, was utterly overthrown.
2. Uncle of Cneius Pompeius Magnus, not in political life, but celebrated for his proficiency in geometry, jurisprudence, and philosophy. He was a Stoic.

good; and in close alliance with justice, beneficence, which may also be called benignity or liberality. The first demand of justice is, that no one do harm to another, unless provoked by injury;[1] the next, that one use common possessions as common, private, as belonging to their owners. Private possessions, indeed, are not so by nature, but by ancient occupancy, as in the case of settlers in a previously uninhabited region; or by conquest, as in the territory acquired in war; or by law, treaty, agreement, or lot.[2] Thus it comes to pass that the territory of Arpinas is said to belong to the Arpinates, that of Tusculum to the Tuscans, and a similar account is to be given of the possessions of individual owners. Because each person thus has for his own a portion of those things which were common by nature, let each hold undisturbed what has fallen to his possession. If any one endeavors to obtain more for himself, he will violate the law of human society. But since, as it has been well said by Plato, we are not born for ourselves alone; since our country claims a part in us, our parents a part, our friends a part; and since, according to the Stoics, whatever the earth bears is created for the use of men, while men were brought into being for the sake of men, that they might do good to one another,—in this matter we ought to follow nature as a guide, to contribute our part to the common good, and by the interchange of kind offices, both in giving and receiving, alike by skill, by labor, and by the resources at our command, to strengthen the social union of men among men. But the foundation of justice is good faith, that is, steadfastness and truth in promises and agreements. Hence, though it may seem to some too far-fetched, I may venture to imitate the Stoics in their painstaking inquiry into the origin of words, and to derive *faith*[3] from the *fact* corresponding to the promise.

Of injustice there are two kinds,—one, that of those who inflict injury; the other, that of those who do not, if they can, repel injury from those on whom it is inflicted. Moreover, he who, moved by anger or by some disturbance of mind, makes an unjust assault on any person, is

1. This exception is one of the few points of discrepancy between the Ciceronian ethics and the moral precepts of Christianity.
2. The veterans who settled on the public lands (*coloni*) received their portions of land by lot, and when a limited number from a particular corps were to be colonized, the persons to be colonized were determined by lot.
3. *Fides*, from *fit* quod *dictum* est, a derivation certainly very improbable, but hardly more so than the derivation from πίστις, or, in the Aeolic dialect, πίττις, which most lexicographers assign to *fides*.

as one who lays violent hands on a casual companion; while he who does not, if he can, ward off or resist the injury offered to another, is as much in fault as if he were to desert his parents, or his friends, or his country. Indeed, those injuries which are purposely inflicted for the sake of doing harm, often proceed from fear, he who meditates harm to another apprehending that, if he refrains, he himself may suffer harm. But for the most part men are induced to injure others in order to obtain what they covet; and here avarice is the most frequent motive.

8. Wealth is sought sometimes for the necessary uses of life, sometimes for indulgence in luxury. In those possessed of a higher order of mind the desire for money is entertained with a view to the increase of the means of influence and the power of generous giving. Thus, not long ago, Marcus Crassus[1] pronounced no property sufficient for one who meant to hold a foremost place in the republic, unless its income would enable him to support an army. Others, again, delight in magnificent furniture, and in an elegant and profuse style of living. In all these ways there has come to be an unbounded desire for money. Nor, indeed, is the increase of property, without harm to any one, to be blamed; but wrong-doing for the sake of gain is never to be tolerated. Most of all, however, large numbers of persons are led to lose sight of justice by the craving for military commands, civic honors, and fame. The saying of Ennius,

> *"Where kingship is concerned,*
> *No social bond or covenant is sacred,"*

has a much broader application; for, as to whatever is of such a nature that but few can be foremost in it, there is generally so keen a rivalry that it is exceedingly difficult to keep social duty inviolate. This was recently illustrated by the audacity of Caius Caesar, who overturned all laws, human and divine, to obtain the sovereignty which he had

---

1. Surnamed Dives. He inherited this *cognomen*, and belonged to the fifth generation of the *gens* Licinius that had borne it. His prime ambition seems to have been to verify his name. Pliny says that the estates which he owned outside of Rome amounted in value to two hundred millions of sesterces, equivalent to little less than eight millions of dollars, no account being taken of the much greater value of money then than now. He was a man of respectable ability, of no mean reputation as an orator, and of considerable executive capacity; but it was probably his wealth that gave him his place in the triumvirate with Caesar and Pompey, and that thus procured for him the command in the Parthian war, in which he lost his army and his life.

shaped for himself in the vagaries of his fancy. In this respect it is indeed unfortunate that it is, for the most part, in the greatest minds and in men of transcendent genius that the desire for offices civil and military, for power and for fame, is rife. The more heed, therefore, is to be taken against criminal conduct in this matter.

But in every form of injustice it makes a very essential difference whether the wrong be committed in some disturbance of mind, which is generally brief and temporary, or whether it be done advisedly, and with premeditation. For those things which are done from some sudden impulse are more venial than what is done with plan and forethought. Enough has now been said with regard to the infliction of injury.

9. For omitting to defend the injured, and thus abandoning duty, there are many reasons in current force. Men are sometimes unwilling to incur the enmity, or the labor, or the cost involved in such defence; or by mere carelessness, indolence, sloth, or engrossment in pursuits or employments of their own, they are so retarded in their movements as to leave undefended those whom they ought to protect. It will thus be seen that Plato is not entirely in the right when he says of philosophers, that because they are engaged in the investigation of truth, and because they despise and count as naught what most persons eagerly seek and are always ready to fight with each other for, they are therefore just men.[1] They indeed attain one part of justice, in injuring no one: they fail as to the other part; for, kept inactive by their zeal for learning, they forsake those whom they ought to defend. Plato thinks, too, that they will take no part in public affairs, unless by compulsion. But it were more fitting that they should do this of their own accord; for the very thing which it is right to do, can be termed virtuous only if it be voluntary. There are, also, those who, either from the over-anxious care of their property or from misanthropic feeling, profess to confine their attention to their own affairs, so as to avoid even the appearance of doing injury to any one. They are free from one kind of injustice: they fall into the other; for they forsake social duty, inasmuch as they bestow upon it neither care, nor labor, nor cost. Since, then, we have assigned to each of the two kinds of injustice its inducing causes, having previously determined the constituent elements of justice, we shall easily ascertain the specific duty of any particular occasion, unless we be blinded by inordinate self-love. However, the care of other

---

1. This is the substance of a discussion in the 6th Book of Plato's Republic.

men's concerns is difficult. Although Chremes, in Terence's play, thinks nothing human indifferent to him, yet because we perceive and feel the things, prosperous or adverse, which happen to ourselves more keenly than those that happen to others, which we see, as it were, at a great distance, we decide concerning them otherwise than we should concerning ourselves in like case. Therefore those give good counsel who forbid our doing that as to the equity of which we have any doubt. For equity is self-evident; doubt implies a suspicion of wrong.

10. But there are frequent occasions when those things which are generally regarded as worthy of a just man, and one of good report, such as the restoring of a trust or the fulfilment of a promise, are reversed, and become the opposite of right, and what belongs to truth and good faith seems to change its bearing, so that justice demands its violation. Here reference is fittingly made to what I have laid down as the fundamental principles of justice, first, that injury should be done to no one, and in the next place, that service should be rendered to the common good. When these principles are modified by circumstances, duty is also modified, and is not always the same. There may perchance be some promise or agreement, the fulfilment of which is harmful to him to whom the promise was made or to him who made it. Thus, to take an instance from the popular mythology, if Neptune had not kept his promise to Theseus,[1] Theseus would not have been bereft of his son, Hippolytus; for, of the three wishes which Neptune had promised to grant him, the third, as the story runs, was his demand in anger for the death of Hippolytus, the granting of which plunged him into the deepest sorrow. Promises, then, are not to be kept, when by keeping them you do harm to those to whom they are made; nor yet if they injure you more than they benefit him to whom you made them, is it contrary to duty that the greater good should be preferred to the less.[2] For instance, if you engaged to appear as an advocate in an

---

1. Among the myths as to the parentage of Theseus, there is one which makes him the son of Poseidon, or Neptune, who was said to have promised to grant him three wishes, two of which had already been granted, when Phaedra, his wife, accused her step-son Hippolytus of an attempted criminal intrigue with her. Theseus claimed of Poseidon his son's destruction, and Poseidon accordingly sent a bull from the water to frighten the horses of Hippolytus, as he was driving in his chariot by the sea-shore. The horses upset the chariot, and dragged Hippolytus till he died. Theseus too late ascertained that his son was innocent, and that his wife had falsely accused him because he had repulsed her advances toward a criminal intimacy.

2. The Hebrew conception of righteousness, "He that sweareth to his own hurt and

impending lawsuit, and meanwhile your child became severely ill, you would not fail in your duty to your client by breaking your promise; on the other hand, he to whom you made the promise would be false to his duty, if he complained of your deserting him. Again, who does not perceive that promises extorted by fear,[1] or obtained by fraud, are not to be kept? Indeed, such promises are made void, in most cases by praetorian edict,[2] in some by express statutes.

There are, also, wrongs committed by a sort of chicanery, which consists in a too subtle, and thus fraudulent, interpretation of the right. Hence comes the saying: The extreme of right is the extreme of wrong. Under this head, there have been many violations of the right in the administration of public affairs, as in the case of him who, during a thirty days' truce with an enemy, ravaged the enemy's territory by night, on the pretext that the truce had been agreed upon for so many days, not nights.[3] Nor can we approve of our fellow-citizen, if the story is true, that Quintus Fabius Labeo, or some one else,—I know of the matter only by hearsay,—being appointed by the Senate as an umpire between the people of Nola and those of Neapolis about their boundaries, when he came to the spot, argued with each party separately that they should not be greedy or covetous, but should rather recede than advance in their demands of each other. When they had both complied with his advice, there remained some territory between these previously contiguous states; and so he fixed their bounds in accordance with their respective claims, and adjudged the intermediate territory to the

changeth not," is certainly in closer accordance with the absolute right than this maxim of Cicero. Yet Cicero's example under this head really belongs to another category, that of circumstances so altered as in the very nature of the case to make a promise void.

1. A promise wrong in itself cannot be rightfully made, even under stress of fear; and if made, should not be kept; for two wrongs cannot make a right. But a promise which one has a right to make, as that of a ransom for one's life, is sacred in the forum of conscience, if not binding in law. If a man regards his life as worth a certain price, and offers that price, there is no rightful reason why he should not pay it.

2. The *praetor urbanus* was virtually the chief justice of Rome. On entering upon the duties of his office he published a manifesto, or *edictum*, stating the principles to be recognized by him in the interpretation and application of the laws. The principles laid down in these successive edicts, and those involved in praetorian decisions under them, unless abrogated or nullified by express legislation, were regarded as having the force of law, and corresponded to what we familiarly term judge-made law.

3. There are two transactions of this kind on record,—one of Cleomenes, the Spartan king, in a war with Argos; the other, of the Thracians, when at war with the Boeotians.

Roman people.[1] This, indeed, is swindling, not arbitration. Shrewdness like this is to be shunned in transactions of every kind.

11. There are also certain duties to be observed toward those who may have injured you. For there is a limit to revenge and punishment,—nay, I know not whether it may not be enough for him who gave the provocation to repent of his wrong-doing, so that he may not do the like again, and that others may be the less disposed to do as he has done. In the public administration, also, the rights of war are to be held sacred. While there are two ways of contending, one by discussion, the other by force, the former belonging properly to man, the latter to beasts, recourse must be had to the latter if there be no opportunity for employing the former. Wars, then, are to be waged in order to render it possible to live in peace without injury; but, victory once gained, those are to be spared who have not been cruel and inhuman in war, as our ancestors even admitted to citizenship the Tuscans, the Aequi, the Volsci, the Sabines, the Hernici; while they utterly destroyed Carthage and Numantia. I could wish that they had not destroyed Corinth; but I believe that they had some motive, especially the convenience of the place for hostile movements,—the fear that the very situation might be an inducement to rebellion.[2] In my opinion, peace is always to be sought when it can be made on perfectly fair and honest conditions. In this matter had my opinion been followed, we should now have, not indeed the best republic possible, but a republic of some sort, which is no longer ours. Still further, while those whom you conquer are to be kindly treated, those who, laying down their arms, take refuge in the good faith of the commander of the assailing army, ought to be received to quarter, even though the battering-ram have already shaken their walls.[3] In this respect justice used to be so carefully observed by our people, that by the custom of our ancestors those who received into allegiance states or nations subdued in war were their patrons. Indeed, the rights of war are prescribed with the most sacred care by the fecial

---

1. Quintus Fabius Labeo lived more than a century before Cicero. Valerius Maximus tells the same story, but without expressing any doubt as to the name of the umpire. He adds that the same Labeo, after a victory over Antiochus, King of Macedonia, having made peace on condition of the surrender of half of the king's fleet, cut all the vessels into halves, so as utterly to destroy the fleet.

2. Corinth had two ports,—one commanding the Ionian, the other the Aegean sea.

3. It was the established custom of the Romans to admit to quarter enemies who surrendered before the application of the battering-ram to their walls.

law[1] of the Roman people, from which it may be understood that no war is just unless after a formal demand of satisfaction for injury, or after an express declaration and proclamation of hostilities. Popilius, as commander, held control of a province. A son of Cato served his first campaign in his army. When Popilius saw fit to discharge one of the legions, he discharged also Cato's son, who served in that same legion. But when the youth remained in the army for love of military service, Cato wrote to Popilius that if he permitted his son to stay, he must make him take a second oath of military duty, else, the term of the first oath having expired, he could not lawfully fight with the enemy. Thus there used to be the most scrupulous observance of the right in the conduct of war. There is, indeed, extant a letter of Marcus Cato the elder to his son Marcus, in which he writes that he has heard of his son's discharge by the consul, after service in Macedonia in the war with Perseus, and warns him not to go into battle, inasmuch as it is not right for one who is no longer a soldier to fight with the enemy.[2]

12. In this connection it occurs to my mind that in the early time the name denoting an enemy engaged in actual war was the word employed to denote a foreigner, the unpleasantness of the fact being thus relieved by the mildness of the term; for he whom we call a foreigner bore with our ancestors the appellation which we now give to an enemy. The laws of the Twelve Tables show this, as, for instance, "A day assigned for trial with a foreigner," "Perpetual right of ownership as against a foreigner."[3] What can more truly indicate gentleness of spirit than

---

1. So called from the *fetiales*,—priests whose duty it was, as heralds, to perform all the ceremonies connected with the declaration of war, the ratifying of peace, and the making of treaties. These forms were regarded as religious solemnities.

2. Commentators in general see here two versions of the same story, and suppose one of the two to be spurious. Yet there is no reason other than the internal evidence for rejecting either, and they may both be true of the same Cato and the same son. The Ligurian war in which Popilius was commander occurred four years before the war with Perseus. In the former, Marcus Cato the younger may have made his first campaign, and in the latter, though no longer a *tiro* or novice in the art of war, he may have been discharged as before, and his father have repeated his legal objection to the son's continuous service.

3. This passage can be literally rendered only by retaining the Latin terms employed, as thus: "He who by our present usage would be called *perduellis* was in former time called *hostis*, the unpleasantness of the fact being thus relieved by the mildness of the term; for him whom we now term *peregrinus* our ancestors called *hostis*. The laws of the Twelve Tables show this, as, for instance, 'A day assigned for trial *cum hoste*,' 'Perpetual right of ownership *adversus hostem*.'" In extant Latin literature the use of *hostis* in the sense of *enemy* seems to have been nearly, if not quite, universal. There is, indeed, a passage in Plautus in which the word is evidently used in the sense of *foreigner*; but this

calling him with whom you are at war by so mild a name? Yet time
has made that word harsher; for it has ceased to denote a foreigner,
and has retained, as properly belonging to it, its application to an
adversary in arms. Even when there is a contest for power, and fame
is sought in war, there ought still to underlie the conflict the same
grounds that I have named above as just causes for war. But the wars
waged for superiority in honor or in dominion should be conducted
with less bitterness of feeling than where there are actual wrongs to
be redressed. For as we contend with a fellow-citizen in one way if
he is an enemy, in a very different way if he is a rival,—the contest
with the latter being for honor and promotion, with the former for
life and reputation,—so our wars with the Celtiberi and the Cimbri
were waged as with enemies, to determine not which should come
off conqueror, but which should survive; while with the Latins, the
Sabines, the Samnites, the Carthaginians, Pyrrhus, the contest was for
superiority. The Carthaginians, indeed, violated their treaties; Hannibal
was cruel; the others were more worthy of confidence. Indeed, what
Pyrrhus said about restoring the captives of war is admirable:—

> "I ask that you should give no gold, no price;
> In war I ply no trade but sword with sword;
> With steel, and not with gold, stake we our lives.
> Wills queenly Fortune you or I should rule,
> Try we by might. And bear this message with you,—
> For those whose prowess Fortune spared in battle
> Freedom is also spared by my decree.
> Lead them away,—I grant,—the gods approve."[1]

---

appears to be a reference to the title in the law of the Twelve Tables cited above, *status
dies cum hoste.* It seems by no means unlikely that the two meanings of *hostis* may have
co-existed in early use. *Hostis* probably is derived from the same root with ἑστία (whence
comes Vesta), a *hearth*, or—what was the same thing as to the rites of domestic worship—
an altar; and if so, *hostis* might mean either a *stranger* to be received to the hospitality
of the hearth, or an *enemy* to be made a victim at the altar. *Hostia*, an animal sacrificed,
and *hostire*, to strike, throw light upon this last meaning. Some of the old lexicographers,
including no less a man than Scaliger, derive *hostis* from the pronoun ὅστις, *whoever*, i.e.,
any person whatsoever outside of one's own family, neighborhood, or nation, a stranger,
and therefore, *prima facie* an enemy. With this derivation—which I do not regard as
valid—the two meanings of *hostis* might have been coeval and concurrent.

1. These verses are from the "Annales" of Ennius, and are supposed to be addressed
to the deputies sent with a large sum of money to treat with Pyrrhus for the release of
prisoners after the battle of Heraclea, B. C. 280.

A sentiment truly royal, and worthy of the race of the Aeacidae.[1]

13. Still further, if any person, induced by stress of circumstances, makes a promise to a public enemy, good faith must be observed in keeping such a promise. Thus Regulus, in the first Punic war, taken captive by the Carthaginians, sent to Rome to negotiate an exchange of prisoners, and bound by an oath to return, in the first place, on his arrival, gave his opinion in the Senate that the prisoners should not be sent back, and then, when his kindred and friends tried to retain him, preferred returning to punishment to breaking his faith with the enemy.

But in the second Punic war, after the battle of Cannae, the ten men whom Hannibal sent to Rome bound by an oath that they would return unless they obtained the redemption of the prisoners of war, were all disfranchised for life[2] by the censors, because they had perjured themselves. Nor did that one of the ten escape who had incurred guilt by the fraudulent performance of his oath. He, having been suffered by Hannibal to leave the camp, returned shortly afterward, saying that he had forgotten something. Then going out again from the camp, he imagined himself acquitted of his oath, and he was so in words alone, not in fact. But in a promise, what you mean, not what you say, is always to be taken into account. The most illustrious example of justice toward an enemy was presented by our ancestors, when the Senate and Caius Fabricius sent back to Pyrrhus a deserter who promised the Senate to kill the king by poison. Thus they refused to sanction the murder of an enemy, and a powerful one, and one who was making war on them without provocation.

Enough has now been said about duties connected with war.

We should also bear it in mind that justice is to be maintained even toward those of the lowest condition. But the lowest condition and fortune is that of slaves, who, it has been well said, ought to be treated as hired servants, to have their daily tasks assigned them, and to receive a just compensation for their labor.[3] In fine, while wrong may be done

---

1. The kings of Epeirus claimed to be lineal descendants of Aeacus, the son of Zeus, who for the righteousness of his rule on earth was made judge in the under-world.

2. Literally, left among the *aerarii*, i.e., liable to taxation, but without the rights of citizenship.

3. The Stoics deduced the obligation to treat slaves humanely from their doctrine of human equality, and the indifference of outward conditions to the truly philosophic mind. Seneca goes in this direction to as great length as that of modern anti-slavery reformers. Cicero was an eminently humane master.

in two ways, either by force or by fraud, the latter seems to belong, as it were, to the fox, the former to the lion, and neither to be congenial with man. Yet of the two, fraud is the most detestable. But of all forms of injustice, none is more heinous than that of the men who, while they practise fraud to the utmost of their ability, do it in such a way that they appear to be good men. Enough has been said about justice.

14. In the next place, as was proposed, let us speak of beneficence and liberality, than which, indeed, nothing is more in harmony with human nature; yet at many points it demands circumspection. In the first place, care must be taken lest our kindness be of disadvantage to those whom we seem to benefit, or to others; in the next place, lest our generosity exceed our means; still further, that our benefactions be apportioned to the merit of our beneficiaries,—a fundamental principle of justice to which reference should be had in whatever we do for others. Now, those who bestow on any person what is likely to be of disadvantage to him to whom they seem to be kind, are to be regarded not as beneficent and liberal, but as harmful flatterers; and those who injure some that they may be generous to others, are as much in the wrong as if they directly converted what belongs to others into their own property. Yet there are many, especially those greedy for show and fame, who take from some what they mean to lavish on others, and these persons think that they shall seem beneficent toward their friends if they enrich them, no matter how. But this is so remote from duty, that nothing can be more contrary to duty. We must, then, take care that in our generosity, while we do good to our friends, we injure no one. Therefore the transfer of property by Lucius Sulla and Caius Caesar[1] from its rightful owners to those to whom it did not belong ought not to be deemed generous; for nothing is generous that is not at the same time just. The second caution is that our generosity should not exceed our means; for those who want to be more generous than their property authorizes them to be, in the first place are blameworthy because they are unjust toward their nearest kindred, giving to strangers what ought to be employed for the needs of their own families or bequeathed for their future use. There is, too, connected with generosity of this type, in almost every

---

1. Reference is here made to the vast amount of property confiscated by Sulla from the victims of his proscription, and bestowed with lavish prodigality on his partisans, and to the rich spoils of the provinces which Caesar largely employed to purchase and reward adherents, and to win the popular favor.

instance, a disposition to seize and appropriate wrongfully the property of other men, in order to furnish means for prodigal giving. We can see, also, that a large number of persons, less from a liberal nature than for the reputation of generosity, do many things that evidently proceed from ostentation rather than from good will. It was said, in the third place, that in beneficence regard should be had to merit, in which matter we should take into consideration the character of the candidate for our favor, his disposition toward us, the degree of his familiarity and intimacy with us, and the good offices which he may have previously rendered for our benefit. That all these reasons for our kindness should be combined, is desirable; if some of them are wanting, preponderant weight must be given to the more numerous and more important reasons.

15. But since we pass our lives, not among perfect and faultlessly wise men,[1] but among those in whom it is well if there be found the semblance of virtue, it ought, as I think, to be our purpose to leave none unbefriended in whom there is any trace of virtue; but at the same time those have the highest claim to our kind offices who are most richly endowed with the gentler virtues, moderation, self-control, and this very justice about which I have said so much. For in a man not perfect or wise, a bold and ambitious mind is generally too impetuous; while the virtues that I have just named seem to be more in accordance with the character of a truly good man. Thus far I have spoken only of the character of those to whom our kind offices are to be rendered. In the next place, as to the good will borne to us, our first duty is to bestow the most on those who hold us in the dearest regard. We ought, however, to judge of their good will not, as young people often do, by ardent expressions of love, but rather by the firmness and constancy of their attachment. But if there are obligations on our part, so that kindness is not to begin with us, but to be returned by us, there is all the greater responsibility laid upon us; for there is no more essential duty than that of returning kindness received. If Hesiod bids us to restore what we have borrowed for use in a greater measure, if we can, what ought we to do when appealed to by unsolicited beneficence? Ought we not to imitate fertile fields, which bring forth much more than they received? If we do not hesitate to confer favors on those who, we hope, will be

---

1. The Stoics maintained that the truly wise man lived only in theory, but had had no actual being in this world.

of service to us, what ought we to be toward those who have already done us service? For while there are two kinds of generosity, one that of bestowing, the other that of returning good offices,—whether we bestow or not, it is for us to choose; but to omit the returning of kindness is impossible for a good man, if he can do so without wronging any one. But there is room for discrimination as to the benefits received; nor can it be denied that the greater the benefit, the greater is the obligation. In this matter the first thing to be considered is, with what degree of earnestness, zeal, and true benevolence one has shown us kindness. For many bestow benefits at haphazard, without judgment or method, or roused to action by some sudden impulse of mind, as if by a blast of wind; and their kindnesses are not to be esteemed so great as those which are conferred with judgment, deliberately and continuously. But alike in bestowing benefit and in returning kindness, other things being equal, it is in the highest degree incumbent upon us to do the most for those who need the most. The contrary is the common habit. Him from whom men hope the most, even if he has no need, they are the most ready to serve.

16. Still further, human society and fellowship will be best maintained, if where there is the most intimate relation, the greatest amount of kindness be bestowed. Here it may be well to trace back the social relations of men to their principles in nature. The first of these principles is that which is seen in the social union of the entire race of man. Its bond is reason as expressed in language,[1] which by teaching, learning, imparting, discussing, deciding, conciliates mutual regard, and unites men by a certain natural fellowship; nor in any respect are we farther removed from the nature of beasts, in which, we often say, there is courage, as in the horse and the lion, but not justice, equity, goodness, inasmuch as they have neither reason nor language. Indeed, it is through this society, so broadly open to men with one another, to all with all, that common possession is to be maintained as to whatever nature has produced for the common use of men; so that while those things that are specially designated by the statutes and the civil law are held as thus decreed, according to these very laws other things may be regarded in the sense of the Greek proverb, "All things are common among friends." Indeed, all those things seem to be common among

---

1. In the Latin, *ratio et oratio*,—a verbal assonance which our language affords us no means of translating.

men, which are of the kind designated by Ennius in a single example,
but comprehending many others:—

> *"Who kindly shows a wanderer his way,*
> *Lights, as it were, a torch from his own torch,—*
> *In kindling others' light, no less he shines."*

This one instance suffices to illustrate the rule, that whatever one can
give without suffering detriment should be given even to an entire
stranger. Thus among common obligations we may reckon, to prohibit
no one from drinking at a stream of running water; to permit any one
who wishes to light fire from fire; to give faithful advice to one who is in
doubt,—which things are useful to the receiver, and do no harm to the
giver. But since the resources of individuals are small, while the multitude of those who need them is unbounded, this indiscriminate giving
should have the limit suggested by Ennius, "No less he shines," so that
we may have the means of generosity to those peculiarly our own.

17. But there are several degrees of relationship among men. To
take our departure from the tie of common humanity, of which I have
spoken, there is a nearer relation of race, nation, and language, which
brings men into very close community of feeling. It is a still more intimate bond to belong to the same city; for the inhabitants of a city have in
common among themselves forum, temples, public walks, streets, laws,
rights, courts, modes and places of voting, beside companionships and
intimacies, engagements and contracts, of many with many. Closer still
is the tie of kindred; for by this from the vast society of the human race
one is shut up into a small and narrow circle. Indeed, since the desire
of producing offspring is common by nature to all living creatures, the
nearest association consists in the union of the sexes;[1] the next, in the
relation with children; then, that of a common home and a community
of such goods as appertain to the home. Then the home is the germ of
the city, and, so to speak, the nursery of the state. The union of brothers
comes next in order, then that of cousins less or more remote, who,
when one house can no longer hold them all, emigrate to other houses
as if to colonies. Then follow marriages[2] and affinities by marriage, thus

---

1. Latin, *conjugium*, which is often employed to denote marriage without religious
ceremonies, and not necessarily permanent, and is used equally as to men and the lower
animals.

2. Latin, *connubia*, which denotes legal marriages, deemed sacred and permanent as
compared with *conjugia*.

increasing the number of kindred. From this propagation and fresh growth of successive generations states have their beginning. But the union of blood, especially, binds men in mutual kindness and affection; for it is a great thing to have the same statues of ancestors, the same rites of domestic worship, the same sepulchres. But of all associations none is more excellent, none more enduring, than when good men, of like character, are united in intimacy. For the moral rectitude of which I have so often spoken, even if we see it in a stranger, yet moves us, and calls out our friendship for him in whom it dwells. Moreover, while every virtue attracts us to itself, and makes us love those in whom it seems to exist, this is emphatically true of justice and generosity. At the same time, nothing is more lovable, and nothing brings men into more intimate relations, than the common possession of these moral excellences; for those who have the same virtuous desires and purposes love one another as they love themselves, and they realize what Pythagoras would have in friendship, the unifying of plurality. That also is an intimate fellowship which is created by benefits mutually bestowed and received, which, while they give pleasure on both sides, produce a lasting attachment between those who thus live in reciprocal good offices. But when you survey with reason and judgment the entire field of human society, of all associations none is closer, none dearer, than that which unites each of us with our country. Parents are dear, children are dear, so are kindred and friends; but the country alone takes into her embrace all our loves for all, in whose behalf what good man would hesitate to encounter death, if he might thus do her service? The more detestable is the savageness of those who by every form of guilt have inflicted grievous wounds on their country, and are and have been employed in her utter subversion. Now, if you make an estimate and comparison[1] of the degree of service to be rendered in each relation, the first place must be given to our country and our parents, bound as we are to them by paramount benefits; next come our children, and the entire family which looks to us alone, nor in stress of need can have any other refuge; then, afterward, the kindred with whom we are on pleasant terms, and with whom, for the most part, we are in the same condition of life. For the reasons indicated

---

1. Latin, *contentio et comparatio*, literally, a stretching of two or more objects side by side, and measuring their equality or nonequality in length,—a figure which can hardly be represented in translation.

we owe chiefly to these that I have named the necessary protection of daily life; but companionship, conviviality, counsel, conversation, advice, consolation, sometimes reproof also, have their most fruitful soil in friendship, and that is the most pleasant friendship which is cemented by resemblance in character.

18. In discharging all these duties, we ought to consider what is most needful for each person, and what each person either can or cannot obtain without our aid. Thus the degrees of relationship will not correspond with those of the occasions for our kind offices; and there are duties which we owe to some rather than to others, on grounds independent of their connection with us. Thus you would help a neighbor rather than a brother or an intimate friend in harvesting his crops; while in a case in court you would appear as an advocate for your kinsman or friend rather than for your neighbor. These and similar points are to be carefully considered in every department of duty, and we should practise and exercise ourselves so that we may be good calculators of duty, and by adding and subtracting may ascertain the remainder, and thus know how much is due to each person. Indeed, as neither physicians, nor commanders, nor orators, though they understand the rules of their art, can accomplish anything worthy of high commendation without practice and exercise; so, though the precepts for the faithful discharge of duty be delivered, as I am delivering them now, the very greatness of the work which they prescribe demands practice and exercise. I have now shown, with nearly sufficient fulness of detail, how the right, on which duty depends, is derived from the constituent elements of human society.

It is to be observed that of the four sources from which right and duty flow, the greatest admiration attends that consisting in a large and lofty mind which looks down on human fortunes. Thus, when reproach is intended, nothing occurs more readily than utterances like this,—

> "Ye, youths, indeed show but a woman's soul;
> That heroine, a man's;"—

or this,—

"Give, Salmacis,[1] spoils without sweat and blood."[2]

On the other hand, in panegyrics, our speech rolls on with a fuller flow when we praise deeds that have been wrought with a large mind, bravely and grandly. Hence the field for eloquent discourse about Marathon, Salamis, Plataea, Thermopylae, Leuctrae; hence the fame of our own fellow-countrymen, Cocles, the Decii, Cneius and Publius Scipio; hence the glory of Marcus Marcellus, and of others more than can be numbered; and the Roman people, as a nation, excels other nations chiefly in this very greatness of soul. In particular, the prevailing love for glory in war is manifested in the almost uniform clothing of statues in military attire.[3]

19. But this loftiness of spirit, manifested in peril and in toil, if devoid of justice, and contending for selfish ends, not for the public good, is to be condemned; for not only does it not appertain to virtue,—it belongs rather to a savageness that spurns all human feelings.[4] Therefore courage is well defined by the Stoics as the virtue that contends for the right. No one, then, who has sought a reputation for courage by treachery and fraud, has won the fame he sought. Nothing that is devoid of justice can be honorable. It was well said by Plato: "Not only is knowledge, when divorced from justice, to be termed subtlety rather than wisdom; but also the soul prompt to encounter danger, if moved thereto by self-interest, and not by the common good, should have the reputation of audacity rather than of courage." Therefore I would have brave and high-spirited men also good and simple, friends of truth, remote from guile,—traits of character which belong to the very heart of justice. But the mischief is, that in this exaltation and largeness of soul obstinacy and an excessive lust of power very easily have birth. For as, according to Plato, the entire character of the Lacedaemonians was set

---

1. Salmacis was the name of a fountain in Caria, so called from a not very virtuous nymph of that name. The waters of the fountain were said to enervate those who bathed in it, and it was fabled to have been the resort of eager pleasure-seekers of both sexes. Trophies were, of course, won there by wanton dalliance, and not by deeds of prowess.

2. Some commentators say that these scraps of verse are from Ennius; others say that it is not known whence they come. The latter are probably in the right.

3. There were hardly any distinguished Romans that had not held some military command, so that even for those best known as civilians a military costume might not have been inappropriate.

4. Latin, *immanitatis* omnem *humanitatem* repellentis,—one of those untranslatable assonances in which Cicero delights, and which contribute largely to the euphony of his diction.

on fire by the desire for victory, so now, in proportion as one surpasses others in grandeur of soul, he is ambitious to hold the foremost place among those in power, or rather, to rule alone. Now it is hard, when you covet pre-eminence, to maintain the equity which is the most essential property of justice. Hence it is that such men suffer themselves to be overcome neither in debate nor by any legal or constitutional hindrance, and in the state they, for the most part, employ bribery and intrigue that they may acquire the greatest influence possible, and may rise by force, rather than maintain equality with their fellow-citizens by justice. But the greater the difficulty, the greater the glory. Nor is there any occasion that ought to be devoid of justice. Therefore not those who inflict, but those who repel, wrong ought to be deemed brave and magnanimous. A soul truly and wisely great regards the right to which the nature of man aspires as consisting in deeds, not in fame; it chooses to be chief rather than to seem so. On the other hand, he who depends on the waywardness of the undiscerning multitude does not deserve to be reckoned among great men. But in proportion to a man's towering ambition, he is easily urged by the greed of fame to deeds averse from justice. His is a slippery standing-ground;[1] for we seldom find a man, who, for labors undertaken and dangers encountered, does not demand fame as the price of his exploits.

20. A brave and great soul is, in fine, chiefly characterized by two things. One of these is the contempt of outward circumstances in the persuasion that a man ought not to admire or wish or seek aught that is not right and becoming, or to yield to human influence, or to passion, or to calamity. The other is that, with this disposition of mind, one should undertake the conduct of affairs great, indeed, and, especially, beneficial, but at the same time arduous in the highest degree, demanding severe toil, and fraught with peril not only of the means of comfortable living, but of life itself. Of these two things, all the lustre and renown, and the utility too, belong to the latter: but their cause and the habit of mind that makes men great lie in the former; for in this is inherent that which renders souls truly great, and lifts them above the vicissitudes of human fortune. Moreover, this first constituent of greatness consists in two things, in accounting the right alone as good, and in freedom from all disturbing passions: for to hold in light esteem, and on fixed and firm principles to despise, objects which to

---

1. On which it is hard to maintain one's moral equipoise.

most persons seem excellent and splendid, is the token of a brave and great soul; and to bear those reputedly bitter experiences which are so many and various in human life and fortunes, in such a way as to depart in no wise from the deportment that is natural to you, in no wise from the dignity befitting a wise man, is the index of a strong mind and of great steadfastness of character. But it is incongruous for one who is not broken down by fear to be broken down by the love of gain, or for him who has shown himself unconquered by labor, to be conquered by sensuality. These failures must be provided against, and the desire for money must especially be shunned. For nothing shows so narrow and small a mind as the love of riches; nothing is more honorable and magnificent than to despise money if you have it not,—if you have it, to expend it for purposes of beneficence and generosity. The greed of fame, also, as I have already said, must be shunned; for it deprives one of liberty, which every high-minded man will strive to the utmost to maintain. Indeed, posts of command[1] ought not to be eagerly sought, nay, they should sometimes rather be refused, sometimes resigned. One should also be free from all disturbing emotions, not only from desire and fear, but equally from solicitude, and sensuality, and anger, that there may be serenity of mind, and that freedom from care which brings with it both evenness of temper and dignity of character. But there are and have been many who, in quest of the serenity of which I am speaking, have withdrawn from public affairs, and taken refuge in a life of leisure. Among these are the most eminent philosophers, including those of the very first rank, and also some stern and grave men, who could not endure the conduct either of the people or of their rulers. Some, too, have taken up their abode in the country, engrossed in the care of their own property. Their design is the same as that of kings, to lack nothing, to obey no one, to enjoy liberty, the essence of which is to live as one pleases.

21. While the purpose of living as one pleases is common to those greedy of power and to the men of leisure of whom I have spoken, the former think that they can realize it if they have large resources; the latter, if they are content with what they have, and with little. Nor is either opinion to be despised. But the life of the men of leisure is easier, and safer, and less liable to give trouble or annoyance to others; while that of those who have fitted themselves for the public service and for

---

1. *Imperia*, by which Cicero, oftener than not, denotes high military office.

the management of large affairs, is more fruitful of benefit to mankind, and more conducive to their own eminence and renown. All things considered, we ought, perhaps, to excuse from bearing part in public affairs those who devote themselves to learning with superior ability, and those who, from impaired health, or for some sufficiently weighty reason, have sought retirement, abandoning to others the power and the praise of civic service. But as for those who have no such reason, yet say that they despise what most persons admire, places of trust and honor in the military or civil service,[1] this, I think, is to be reckoned to their discredit, not to their praise. They, indeed, deserve approval for despising fame and thinking it of no account. But they seem to dread not only toil and trouble, but a certain imagined shame and disgrace from the disappointments and repulses which they must encounter. For there are those who in opposite circumstances fail to act consistently,—who have the utmost contempt for pleasure, yet are unmanned by pain,— who scorn fame, yet are broken down by unpopularity; and these are, indeed, manifest incongruities in a man's character. But those whom nature has endowed with qualities that fit them for the management of public affairs ought, without needless delay, to become candidates for office and to take the interests of the state in charge; for only thus can the state be well governed, and only thus can commanding power of mind be made manifest. At the same time, for those who undertake public trusts, perhaps even more than for philosophers, there is need of elevation of mind, and contempt of the vicissitudes of human fortune, and that serene and unruffled spirit of which I often speak, in order that they may be free from solicitude, and may lead dignified and self-consistent lives. This is easier for philosophers, inasmuch as their condition in life is less open to the assaults of fortune, their wants are fewer, and in case of adverse events they encounter a less heavy fall. On the other hand, those who hold public trusts are obviously liable to stronger mental excitement, and are more heavily burdened with care than those who live in retirement; and they should therefore bring to their duty a corresponding strength of mind, and independence of the ordinary causes of vexation. But let him who meditates entering on any important undertaking, carefully consider, not only whether the undertaking is right, but also whether he has the ability to carry it through; and here he must beware, on the one hand, lest he too readily

---

1. Latin, *imperia et magistratus.*

despair of success from mere want of spirit, or, on the other hand, lest he be over-confident from excessive eagerness. In fine, in all transactions, before you enter upon them, you should make diligent preparation.

22. Moreover, since military achievements are very commonly regarded as outranking civil service, this opinion needs to be refuted; for wars have often been encouraged from the desire of fame, especially by men of superior intellect and genius, when they have the requisite ability for the service of arms, and are ambitious of the places of command which it offers. Yet if we will only look at facts, there have been many civic transactions that have surpassed feats of arms in importance and in renown.[1] Thus, although Themistocles be rightly held in honor, and his name be more illustrious than that of Solon, and Salamis be cited as witness of a most splendid victory which may have a higher place in the popular esteem than Solon's establishing the Areopagus,[2] yet this last must be regarded as no less glorious than the victory. For this was once of benefit; that will always be of benefit to the state, as preserving inviolate the laws of the Athenians and the institutions of their ancestors. And Themistocles could have named no particular in which he could have given help to the Areopagus; while the Areopagus rendered substantial aid[3] to Themistocles, the war having been conducted by the counsel of that same Senate established by Solon. The like may be said of Pausanias[4] and Lysander.[5] Although the common idea is that the Lacedaemonian empire owed its enlargement to their prowess, yet their achievements bear no comparison with the laws and discipline of Lycurgus. For was it not these very institutions that made their armies both more obedient and more courageous? Nor, indeed, when I was a boy, did I regard Marcus Scaurus[6] as inferior

---

1. "Peace hath her victories
No less renowned than war."
Milton, Sonnet xvi.
2. Solon did not establish the Areopagus, which was of even prehistoric origin; but before his time it was merely a criminal court, while he gave it censorial jurisdiction, advisory authority in public affairs, and, in fine, functions that rendered it a council of state, and a strongly conservative force against else unchecked democracy.
3. The Areopagus, in a time of great dearth, furnished funds for the payment of the seamen who were going to fight at Salamis.
4. Pausanias overthrew the Persian general, Mardonius, in the battle of Plataea.
5. Lysander took Athens, and destroyed the Long Walls.
6. Marcus Aemilius Scaurus was a strong conservative and a zealous supporter of the aristocratic party. His deportment, too, was remarkable for its gravity and its general respectability. He may have been a better man than Marius; but he was charged with

to Caius Marius; nor, when I was in public life, did I think Quintus Catulus[1] inferior to Cneius Pompeius.

"Valor abroad is naught, unless at home be wisdom."[2]

Nor yet did Africanus, of rare worth both as a man and as a commander, do greater service to the republic in exterminating Numantia, than at the same time did Publius Nasica, a private citizen, in killing Tiberius Gracchus. This last transaction, indeed, is not wholly of a civil character,—as it was performed by force and arms, it borders on the military; yet it was effected by civic policy without military array. That verse of mine, against which, as I hear, unprincipled and envious men are wont to rail,—

"Let arms yield to the robe, the laurel to the tongue,"[3]

is by no means devoid of excellence. Not to mention others, when I was at the helm of the republic, did not arms yield to the gown? For there was never in the republic greater danger, and never a more profound peace. Thus by my counsels and my assiduity their very weapons fell speedily from the hands of the most audacious citizens. What equally great achievement was ever performed in war? What triumph is to be compared with it? I may take the liberty of boasting to you, my son Marcus, to whom belong both the heritage of this fame and the imitation of my deeds. Forsooth, Cneius Pompeius, a man rich in military renown, in the hearing of many did me the honor of saying that he would in vain have obtained his third triumph, unless by my service to the state he would have had a place for the celebration of his triumph. There are, then, cases of civic courage not inferior to those in war, nay, demanding even a larger amount of labor and of zeal.

---

receiving a heavy bribe from Jugurtha for securing a peace on terms favorable to the king, and he saved himself from penal accountability only by procuring his own appointment as one of the judges for the trial of his accomplices.

1. Quintus Catulus supported Cicero at the time of the Catilinian conspiracy, and was the first in the Senate to hail him as Father of the Country (*pater patriae*).

2. A verse, quoted probably from some lost comedy, the measure being one employed by the comic poets.

3. This verse is from a poem of Cicero on his own times, and mainly to his own glory as carried to its climax in his suppression of the Catilinian conspiracy. It was laughed at for the patent self-conceit which it exhibited.

23. Of a certainty, the virtue which we demand of a lofty and large mind is generated by strength of mind, not of body. Yet the body must be disciplined, and brought into a condition in which it can obey counsel and reason in following out affairs to their issue, and in enduring toil. But the virtue which we demand consists in mental care and thought, in which those who preside over the state in the robe of peace, perform no less service than those who take the lead in war. Indeed, by the counsel of the former, wars have been often prevented or terminated, sometimes, also, begun, as the third Punic war, by the counsel of Marcus Cato,[1] then dead, whose authority outlived him. Therefore skill in the settlement of controversies is more desirable than courage in disputing them by arms; but care must be taken lest we resort to peaceful measures rather to avoid fighting than for the public good.

But war should be undertaken in such a way that it may seem nothing else than a quest of peace. Moreover, it belongs to a brave and firm man not to be disturbed in misfortune, nor to be so thrown off his balance as to be, in the trite phrase, hustled down from his position, but to take prompt thought and counsel, and not to be betrayed into unreason. While as much as this belongs to a great mind, it is also the part of a man of transcendent ability to anticipate the future in thought, and somewhat beforehand to consider what is liable to happen on either side, and what is to be done in case of any possible event, so as not to be compelled at any time to say, "I had not thought of this." Such is the work of a mind large, and lofty, and trusting in discretion and good counsel. But to make rash manoeuvres in battle, and to come to close quarters with the enemy, is something savage and beastlike. Yet when occasion and need demand, there must be hand-to-hand fighting, and death is to be preferred to slavery or poltroonery.

24. As to the destruction and plundering of conquered cities, care must be taken that nothing be done precipitately, nothing cruelly; and it is the part of a truly great man, in times of disorder, to punish the guilty, to spare the many, and, whatever takes place, to keep rectitude and honor inviolate. For as there are those, as I have already said, who prefer military to civil service, so you may find many to whom perilous and hot-headed counsels seem more splendid and imposing than

---

1. As is well known, Cato never gave his vote in the Senate, no matter what the subject, without repeating the words, *Delenda est Carthago*, Carthage must be destroyed. Its destruction took place three years after his death.

calm and deliberate measures. Never, certainly, are we by shunning danger to make ourselves seem tame and timid; but equally are we to avoid encountering needless perils, than which nothing can be more foolish. Therefore, in impending danger, we should imitate the custom of physicians, who employ mild treatment for those but slightly ill, but are compelled to use dangerous and doubtful remedies for severer diseases. Thus it is the part of a madman, in a calm sea to desire a storm with a head-wind; but that of a wise man, to withstand the storm as best he may, especially if the benefits obtained by carrying the matter through successfully are greater than the evil that may be incurred in the conflict. But public transactions are perilous, sometimes to those who undertake them, sometimes to the state; and, again, some run the risk of life, others of fame, and of the good-will of their fellow-citizens. We ought to be more ready to encounter danger for ourselves than for the state, and to contend more promptly for honor and fame than for anything else that concerns ourselves personally.

Yet there have been found many who were ready to pour out not only their money, but even their blood for their country, who would not make the least sacrifice of reputation, even when the well-being of the state demanded it; as, for instance, Callicratidas, who, after having been at the head of the Lacedaemonian forces in the Peloponnesian war, and having repeatedly rendered excellent service, at last reversed everything by rejecting the advice of those who thought it best to remove the fleet from the Arginusae and not to fight with the Athenians. He answered them that the Lacedaemonians, if they lost that fleet, could equip another, while he could not retreat without disgracing himself.[1] This was, indeed, to the Lacedaemonians a blow of moderate severity; that, a ruinous one, by which, when Cleombrotus,[2] for fear of unpopularity, fought rashly with Epaminondas, the power of the Lacedaemonians utterly collapsed. What a contrast here to the advantage of Quintus Maximus,[3] of whom Ennius writes:—

---

1. Callicratidas himself perished in the battle.

2. Cleombrotus was taunted for excess of caution, and was thus induced to risk the battle with the Thebans, against his own judgment. There seems to have been as much hesitation on the Theban side, so that, prior to the battle, the scales would probably have seemed equipoised.

3. Quintus Fabius Maximus, who from his repeatedly avoiding direct conflict with Hannibal in the determination to weary him out by delay, acquired the surname of Cunctator, and has bequeathed the enduring epithet of *Fabian* to a policy like his own.

> *"One man by slow delays restored our fortunes,*
> *Preferring not the people's praise to safety,*
> *And thus his after-glory shines the more."*

This same kind of error is also to be shunned in civil affairs; for there are those who, for fear of unpopularity, dare not say what they think, even if it be the very best that could be said.

25. In fine, let those who are to preside over the state obey two precepts of Plato,—one, that they so watch for the well-being of their fellow-citizens that they have reference to it in whatever they do, forgetting their own private interests; the other, that they care for the whole body politic, and not, while they watch over a portion of it, neglect other portions. For, as the guardianship of a minor, so the administration of the state is to be conducted for the benefit, not of those to whom it is intrusted, but of those who are intrusted to their care. But those who take counsel for a part of the citizens, and neglect a part, bring into the state an element of the greatest mischief, and stir up sedition and discord, some siding with the people, some with the aristocracy, and few being equally the friends of all. From this cause arose great dissensions among the Athenians, and in our republic it has led not only to seditions, but also to destructive civil wars. Partiality of this kind, a citizen who is substantial and brave, and worthy of a chief place in the state, will shun and abhor, and will give himself wholly up to the state, pursuing neither wealth nor power; and he will so watch over the entire state as to consult the well-being of all its citizens. Nor will he expose any one to hatred or envy by false accusation, and he will in every respect so adhere to justice and right as in their behalf to submit to any loss however severe, and to face death itself rather than surrender the principles which I have indicated. Most pitiful in every aspect is the canvassing and scrambling for preferment, of which it is well said by the same Plato, that those who strive among themselves which shall be foremost in the administration of the state, act like sailors who should quarrel for a place at the helm. The same writer exhorts us to regard as enemies those who bear arms against us, not those who desire to care for the interests of the state in accordance with their own judgment, as in the case of the disagreement without bitterness between Publius Africanus and Quintus Metellus.[1]

---

1. They were often on opposite sides in the politics of the city, and sometimes on

Nor are they to be listened to who think that anger is to be cherished toward those who are unfriendly to us on political grounds, and imagine that this betokens a large-minded and brave man; for nothing is more praiseworthy, nothing more befitting a great and eminent man, than placability and clemency. Moreover, in free states and where all have equal rights, there is a demand for courtesy, and for a soul superior to petty causes of vexation, lest if we suffer ourselves to be angry with those who intrude upon us inopportunely, we fall into irritable habits equally harmful and hateful. Yet an easy and accommodating temper is to be approved only so far as may be consistent with the strictness demanded in public business, without which the state cannot be administered. But all punishment and correction ought to be free from personal insult, and should have reference, not to the pleasure of him who administers punishment or reproof, but to the public good. Care also must be taken lest the punishment be greater than the fault, and lest for the same cause some be made penally responsible, and others not even called to account. Most of all is anger to be eliminated in punishment; for he who enters on the office of punishment in anger will never preserve that mean between too much and too little, of which the Peripatetics make so great account,[1] and rightly too, if they only would not commend anger, and say that it is implanted by nature for useful ends. On the other hand, it is under all circumstances to be shunned, and it is desirable that those who preside over the state should be like the laws, which are led to inflict punishment, not by anger, but by justice.

26. Again, in prosperity, and when affairs flow on as we would have them, we should with the utmost care avoid pride, fastidiousness, and arrogance; for it is the token of a frivolous mind to bear either prosperity or adversity otherwise than moderately, and pre-eminently praiseworthy is an equable temperament in one's whole life, the same countenance and the same mien always, as we learn was the case with

---

non-friendly, if not unfriendly terms; but when Africanus was found dead in his bed, and supposed to have been assassinated, Metellus exclaimed, "Come, citizens, to the rescue; the walls of our city are thrown down;" and he ordered his sons to put their shoulders under the bier, saying that they would never have the opportunity to perform that office for a greater man.

1. The Peripatetics, after Aristotle, defined virtue as always consisting of the mean between two extremes. Thus, courage is the mean between rashness and cowardice. The New Academy, to which Cicero belonged, accepted hypothetically the ethics of the Peripatetic school.

Socrates, and equally with Caius Laelius.[1] I regard Philip, king of the Macedonians, though surpassed by his son in achievements and in fame, as having been his superior in affability and kindness. Thus the one was always great, the other often very mean,—so as to give good ground for the rule of those who say that the higher our position is, the more meekly we should carry ourselves. Panaetius, indeed, tells us that Africanus, his pupil and friend, used to say, that as it is common to give horses that, from having been often in battle, rear and prance dangerously, into the hands of professional tamers, that they may be ridden more easily, so men, when at loose reins in prosperity, and over self-confident, should be brought, as it were, to the ring[2] of reason and instruction, that they may fully see the frailty of man's estate, and the fickleness of fortune. Still further, in the extreme of prosperity, especially, resort is to be had to the counsel of friends, and even greater authority to be given to them than under ordinary circumstances. In such a condition we must also take heed lest we open our ears to flatterers, and suffer ourselves to be cajoled. In yielding to sycophancy, we are always liable to be deceived, thinking that we deserve the praise bestowed upon us, whence proceed numberless mistakes, men who are inflated by self-conceit becoming the objects of coarse derision, and committing the most egregious eccentricities in conduct. But enough on this point.

From what has been said, it is to be inferred that the most important affairs, and those indicative of the highest tone of spirit, come under the direction of men in public life, their official duty having the widest scope, and extending to the largest number of persons; but that there are and have been many men of great mind in private life, engaged in important investigations or enterprises, yet attending to no affairs but their own; while others, no less great, midway between philosophers and statesmen, are occupied with the care of their property, not, indeed, increasing it by every means in their power, nor yet depriving their

---

1. Caius Laelius Sapiens, who died before Cicero was born, was a man of but moderate, though not mean reputation as a general, a statesman, and an orator; but had a strong hold on Cicero's veneration as second to no man of his time in elegant culture, especially in Greek literature and philosophy, and also as a stanch advocate of the aristocracy as opposed to the *plebs*. Cicero makes him the chief interlocutor in the *De Amicitia*, and one of the speakers in the *De Senectute* and the *De Republica*.
2. Latin, *gyrum*, the ring or circle, round which horses are ridden to break or tame them.

friends of the benefit of it, but rather, whenever there is need, giving freely to their friends and to the state. Property thus held should, in the first place, have been fairly obtained, and not by any mean or offensive calling; then it should show itself of service to as many as possible, if they only be worthy; then, too, it should be increased by industry and frugality, and should not lie open to the demands of sensuality and luxury rather than to those of generosity and beneficence. He who observes these rules may live in splendor, dignity, and independence, and at the same time with simplicity, with integrity, and in friendly relations with mankind.

27. I have now to speak of the only remaining division of the right, embracing modesty, which gives a certain lustre to life, temperance, discretion, serenity of soul, and moderation in all things. Under this head is included what we may fitly call decorum, or becomingness;[1] the Greeks call it πρέπον.[2] The property of this is that it cannot be separated from the right; for whatever is becoming is right, and whatever is right is becoming. In what way the right and the becoming differ is more easily felt than told; for whatever it is that constitutes becomingness, it makes its appearance when the right has gone before; and thus the becoming is not confined to the division of the right now under discussion, but is equally manifest in the three other divisions. For it is becoming to employ both reason and speech with discretion, and to do what you do deliberately, and on every subject to perceive and discern the truth; and, on the other hand, it is as unbecoming to be deceived, to misjudge, to commit grave mistakes, to be deluded into unwise conduct, as it is to be delirious or insane. Then, too, whatever is just is becoming; on the other hand, whatever is unjust, as it is base, is also unbecoming. The case is the same with courage; for whatever is done manfully and high-spiritedly seems worthy of a man, and becoming; whatever is the opposite of this, as it is base, is also unbecoming. Thus this becomingness of which I speak belongs, indeed, to all virtue, and so belongs to it that it is not discerned by any abstruse process of reasoning, but is perfectly obvious. For there is, in truth, a certain something which is becoming—and it is understood to be contained in every form of

---

1. Literally, what may be called in Latin *decorum*. In what follows I have translated *decorum* by the awkward, yet legitimate word, becomingness, which corresponds in sense very closely to the Latin word, while in making *decorum* an English word we have dropped a part of its native meaning.

2. That which is becoming, or decorous.

virtue—which can be separated from virtue in thought rather than in fact. As grace and beauty of body cannot be separated from health, so this becomingness of which I am speaking is entirely blended with virtue, yet is distinguished from it in conception and thought. It has a twofold definition; for there is a certain general becomingness which has its place in every kind of virtue; and another, subordinate to this and included within it, which belongs to single departments of virtue. The former is usually defined somewhat in this way: That is becoming which is in accordance with the superiority of man in those respects in which his nature differs from that of other animals. The special type included under this general head may be defined as designating that as becoming which is so in accordance with nature as to present the aspect of moderation and self-restraint, together with the air and manner that befit ingenuous breeding.

28. That these things are so understood, we may infer from that becomingness which is the poet's aim, about which I speak more at large in another treatise.[1] We say that poets observe what is becoming, when they represent that which befits each individual character as both done and said. Thus were Aeacus or Minos[2] to say,—

> *"No matter how they hate me while they fear me,"*

or,

> *"The very father is his children's tomb,"*[3]

it would seem unbecoming; for the tradition is that they were just men. But when Atreus[4] so speaks, the audience applaud; for the speech befits the character. Now, the poets will determine from the type of the character in hand, what befits each character. To us, however, Nature has assigned a character endowed with great excellence and superiority over other animals. The poets, on their part, in a great diversity of characters, will determine what is suitable and becoming to each, even to the very worst. But since the parts of consistency, moderation, self-restraint, modesty, are assigned to us by Nature, and since the same

---

1. In the *Orator*.
2. Sons of Jupiter, said to have led such righteous lives that they were made judges in the underworld.
3. These passages are probably from the lost tragedy of Atreus, by Attius.
4. He, in Greek fable, killed the children of his brother Thyestes, and feasted him on their flesh.

Nature teaches us not to be indifferent as to the manner of our conduct
toward men, we may thus see how broad is the scope, both of that
becomingness which belongs to all virtue, and of this which is made
manifest in each several kind of virtue. For as the beauty of the body
attracts notice by the symmetry of the limbs, and gives delight by the
very fact that all its parts harmonize with a certain graceful effect, so
this becomingness which shines in the life calls forth the esteem of
society by the order, consistency, and moderation of all that is said and
done. A certain measure of respect should indeed be shown toward
all men, whether in superior position or on the common level; for
indifference to the opinion of others is the token, not only of self-
sufficiency, but of utter recklessness. But in the treatment of men there
is a difference between justice and courtesy.[1] It is the part of justice
not to injure men; of courtesy, not to give them offence, and it is in
this last that the influence of becomingness is most clearly seen. With
this exposition, I think that the nature of what we term becoming may
be sufficiently understood.

The duty derived from it first leads to conformity with Nature and
observance of her fitnesses, whom if we follow as a leader, we shall
never err, and shall attain equally that which is in its essence keen and
clear-sighted, that which is adapted to human society, and that which
is strong and brave.[2] But the chief province of becomingness is in the
division of virtue now under discussion; for not only movements of the
body fitted to nature, but much more those movements of the mind
which are in harmony with nature, claim approval. The natural constitution of the human mind is twofold. One part consists in impulse,
ὁρμή[3] in Greek, which hurries a man hither and thither; the other, in
reason, which teaches and explains what is to be done and what to be
avoided. Thus it is that reason fitly presides, and impulse obeys.

29. Every purpose ought to be free alike from rashness and from
negligence, nor ought anything to be done for which a reason worthy of
approval cannot be given. This, indeed, is almost a complete definition
of duty.[4] Moreover, the impulses must be made obedient to reason,

---

1. Latin, *verecundia*, which commonly denotes modesty, but here evidently means
that courtesy which is a part or a consequence of modesty.
2. The first three cardinal virtues are thus enumerated.
3. Literally, *impulse*. The Latin word here is *appetitus*, which I have rendered impulse,
because anger and fear are included under it.
4. *Officium*, from *facere ob*, to do on account of, or for a sufficient reason.

and neither get the advance of it, nor yet from stupidity or indolence lag behind it, and they must be quiet and free from all excitement,—a state of things which will show consistency and moderation in their full lustre. For impulses which rove too far, prancing, as it were, either in the pursuit or avoidance of objects within their scope, and not sufficiently held in by reason, evidently transcend bound and measure; for they desert and repudiate obedience, nor do they submit themselves to reason, to which they are subject by the law of nature. By such impulses not only minds, but bodies are thrown into disturbance. You can discriminate at sight the very countenances of the angry, of those who are excited by sensual passion or by fear, or of those who are beside themselves through excess of pleasure, in all of whom face, voice, gait, and posture are changed. Hence,—to return to the delineation of duty,— it is inferred that all the appetites must be checked and calmed, and that watchfulness and care must be on the alert to prevent us from doing anything rashly and at haphazard, inconsiderately and carelessly. For we are not so constituted by nature as to seem made for sport and jest, but rather for sobriety and for certain more weighty and important pursuits. It is, indeed, right to indulge in sport and jest, but only as in sleep and other relaxations, when we have done full justice to grave and serious concerns. Still further, the very style of jesting ought not to be extravagant or immoderate, but in pure taste and with genuine humor. For as we do not give boys the unlimited liberty of play, but only that degree of freedom which is consistent with good conduct, so in jest itself there ought to shine forth something of the radiance of a pure character. There are, in truth, two kinds of jokes,—the one vulgar, impertinent, vicious, obscene; the other, elegant, refined, witty, humorous. This last kind fills not only our own Plautus and the old comedy of the Athenians, but also the books of the Socratic philosophers; and many things of this sort have been wittily said by many persons, as, for instance, those sayings collected by the elder Cato[1] which they call ἀποφθέγματα.[2] The distinction between a refined

---

1. Marcus Porcius Cato, the Censor. This collection is lost; but there are some specimens of its contents in Cicero's *Orator*. Collections of this kind, probably, were not unusual among the ancients, though, so far as I know, but one has been preserved in either of the classic tongues, namely, the Ἀστε[269?]α of Hierocles, the work, probably, of a compiler of whom no other vestige remains.

2. Apophthegms, terse, pithy sayings, including jokes. Lord Bacon's "Apophthegms New and Old" are, all of them, anecdotes comprising smart, pointed sayings, and many of them jokes.

and a vulgar joke is easily made. The one, if not untimely, is worthy of any man at leisure; the other, unworthy of any man above the condition of a slave, if polluted by vile images or filthy words. A certain limit is to be observed in sport, also, lest we run into excess, and, carried away by pleasure, lapse into some kind of disgraceful conduct. Our field[1] for athletic exercises, and the amusement of the chase, furnish proper examples of sport.

30. It is appropriate to every discussion of duty, always to bear in mind how far the nature of man excels that of cattle and other beasts. They feel nothing save sensual pleasure, and toward that they are borne by every instinct; but the mind of man is nourished by learning and reflection, is constantly thinking or doing something, and is led by the pleasure and profit derived from what is seen and heard. And even if one is unduly inclined to sensual pleasure, if he only be not on a level with brute beasts,—for there are some who are men, not in fact, but in name,—if he be ever so little above them, although captivated with the mere delight of the senses, he hides and dissembles the appetite for such pleasure from very shame. Hence it is inferred that bodily pleasure is unworthy of man's superior endowments, and ought to be despised and spurned; and if there be any one who sets some value on sensual gratification, he should carefully keep it within due limits. Thus food and the care of the body should be ordered with reference to health and strength, not to sensual pleasure. Indeed, if we will only bear in mind what excellence and dignity belong to human nature, we shall understand how base it is to give one's self up to luxury, and to live voluptuously and wantonly, and how honorable it is to live frugally, chastely, circumspectly, soberly.

But it is to be borne in mind that we are endowed by nature as it were with two characters, one of which is common to us with other men, inasmuch as we all partake of reason, and of the traits which raise us above the brutes, from which all that is right and becoming is derived, and from which we seek the method of ascertaining our duty; while the other is that which is assigned to each of us individually. For as in bodies there are great dissimilarities,—we see some excelling in speed for the race, others in strength for wrestling; also in personal appearance, some have dignity, others grace,—so in minds there are

---

1. The Campus Martius, used by the Roman youth for riding, driving, swimming, and various athletic sports.

even greater diversities. Lucius Crassus and Lucius Philippus had a great deal of pleasantry; Caius Caesar, the son of Lucius, even more and more elaborate; while in their contemporaries, Marcus Scaurus and Marcus Drusus the younger, there was an unusual severity of manner; in Caius Laelius, much mirthfulness; in his friend Scipio, greater ambition, a more austere type of character. Among the Greeks, too, we have learned that Socrates was pleasant and facetious, and had a jocose way of talking, and meant more than he said, one whom the Greeks call εἴρωνα·[1] on the other hand, that Pythagoras and Pericles obtained the highest authority in their intercourse with men without any seasoning of mirthfulness. We are informed that, of the Carthaginians, Hannibal was crafty, and of our own commanders, that Quintus Maximus readily practised concealment, kept silence, dissembled, laid snares, anticipated the plans of his enemies. In these traits the Greeks assign the foremost place to Themistocles and Jason of Pherae, and accord pre-eminent praise to the cunning and crafty procedure of Solon, who, for his own safety, and that he might render additional service to the state, feigned insanity.[2] There are others of very unlike character, simple and open, who think that nothing should be done covertly or insidiously, votaries of truth, enemies of fraud; others still, who will endure anything whatever, and will be subservient to any one whomsoever, till they attain what they desire, as we saw in the case of Sulla and of Marcus Crassus. Of this class of men we learn that Lysander, the Lacedaemonian, was unsurpassed in crafty plotting and in his power of endurance, while Callicratidas, who succeeded Lysander in the command of the fleet, was of the opposite character. Also in speech, we sometimes see a man of surpassing ability contrive to appear like one of the multitude, as we witnessed in Catulus, both father and son, and in Quintus Mucius Mancia. We have heard from those of an earlier generation that this was the habit of Publius Scipio Nasica, and, on the other hand, that his father, the man who avenged

---

1. The accusative of εἴρων, which literally means a dissembler. Hence our word *irony*, which always involves the idea of a double meaning, and especially of a secondary meaning which shall be latent to the person addressed or satirized, patent to every one else.

2. When Athens had failed in a contest with Megara for the possession of Salamis, a law was passed rendering it criminal to advocate the renewal of the contest. Solon evaded the law by feigning insanity, and recited a poem of his own, calling upon the people to reconquer the "lovely island." The law was repealed, the war renewed, and the island won.

the nefarious enterprises of Tiberius Gracchus, had nothing genial in his address. We learn, too, that Xenocrates, indeed the sternest of philosophers, was on this very score eminent and renowned.[1] There are other innumerable diversities of nature and of manners, which yet give no good ground for obloquy.

31. Every one ought to hold fast, not his faults, but his peculiarities, so as to retain more easily the becomingness which is the subject of our inquiry. We ought, indeed, to act in such a way as shall be in no respect repugnant to our common human nature; yet, holding this sacred, let us follow our individual nature, so that, if there are other pursuits in themselves more important and excellent, we yet may measure our own pursuits by the standard of our own nature. For it is of no avail to resist nature, or to pursue anything which we cannot reach. It is the more apparent of what quality is the becomingness under discussion, when we consider that nothing is becoming that is done, as the phrase is, without Minerva's sanction, that is, with the opposition and repugnancy of nature. In truth, if anything is becoming, nothing surely is more so than uniform consistency in the whole course of life and in each separate action, which you cannot preserve if, imitating the nature of others, you abandon your own. For as we ought to use our native tongue, and not, like some who are perpetually foisting in Greek words, incur well-deserved ridicule, so we ought not to introduce any discordance into our conduct and our general way of living. This difference of natures, indeed, has so much force that sometimes one person ought, and another under the same circumstances ought not, to commit suicide.[2] For was the case of Marcus Cato different from that of the others who surrendered to Caesar in Africa? Yet had they killed themselves, they might perhaps have been worthy of censure, because their mode of life was less severe, and their characters were more pliant; while, since Nature had given Cato an incredible massiveness of character, and he himself had strengthened it by undeviating self-consistency, and had always been steadfast in the purpose once

---

1. Of the traits of personal character described in this section, some are known only on Cicero's authority; while others, attached to well-known names, are matters of history. I have not thought it necessary to give, as I easily might, under the successive names, a series of extracts from a dictionary of classical biography.

2. It is well known that from Zeno, who committed suicide when he thought his life no longer serviceable, down to Seneca, the Stoics maintained the right of suicide as a mode of relief from irretrievable evil, whether bodily disease or untoward circumstances.

conceived and the design once undertaken, it seemed fit for him to die rather than to look upon the face of a tyrant. How many things did Ulysses endure in his long wandering, while he submitted to the service of women,—if Circe and Calypso are to be called women,—and while he strove to be affable and pleasant to all in his whole social intercourse! At home, also, he bore the jeers of slaves and maidservants, that he might attain the object of his desire. But Ajax, with the temper which he is said to have had, would have faced death a thousand times rather than have borne such insults. In view of these things, it will be each man's duty to weigh well what are his own peculiar traits of character, and to keep them in serviceable condition, and not to desire to try how far another man's peculiarities may be becoming to him; for that is most becoming to each man which is most peculiarly his own. Let each of us, then, know his own capacities and proclivities, and show himself a discriminating judge of his own excellences and defects, lest performers on the stage may evince more discretion than we do. For they choose, not the best plays, but those the best adapted to their respective abilities,—those who rely on voice, the Epigoni and Medus; those who depend on action, Menalippa or Clytaemnestra; Rutilius, whom I remember, Antiopa always; Aesopus, not often Ajax.[1] An actor, then, will look to this fitness on the stage; shall not the wise man have equal regard to it in life? Let us therefore bestow our diligence chiefly on those concerns for which we are the best fitted. But if at any time necessity shall have forced us to undertake things outside of our specialty, we must employ all possible care, thought, and diligence, that we may be able to dispose of them, if not becomingly, yet with the least degree of unbecomingness; nor ought we in that case to endeavor to attain capacities not our own, so much as to avoid mistake or failure.

32. To the two characters which, as I have said, every man must sustain, is added a third, imposed upon us by chance, or by circumstances beyond our power; a fourth, also, which we assume at our own discretion. Posts of authority, military commands, high rank, honors, wealth, and their opposites, at the disposal of chance, are controlled by circumstance. But it depends on our own choice what character we

---

1. None of the tragedies here named are extant. It would appear that on the Roman as on the modern stage, actors not only had parts assigned them according to their peculiar types of ability, but that the genius of a leading actor determined the choice of the play in which he should appear.

will assume as to a favorite pursuit or profession. Thus some apply themselves to philosophy; some, to the civil law; some, to oratory; and of the several virtues some prefer to excel in one, some in another. Those, indeed, whose fathers or ancestors have held any special distinction, generally aim at eminence in the same department, as Quintus Mucius, the son of Publius, in the civil law; Africanus, the son of Paulus, in military service. But some add to the honors inherited from their fathers a special reputation of their own, as this very Africanus crowned his military renown by eloquence. Timotheus, the son of Conon, also did the like, being fully his father's equal in military reputation, and adding to it the praise of learning and genius. It is, however, now and then the case that young men, forsaking the example of their ancestors, pursue some plan of their own; and this is the course, almost always, of those who, of obscure origin, set before themselves large aims. All these things ought to be taken into careful consideration when we inquire what is becoming.

At the outset, we should determine in what condition we wish to be, in what kind of pursuits, and whether in private or public life,—a decision the most difficult of all; for it is in early youth, when judgment is the weakest, that one chooses some mode of life with which he has become enamored, and thus is involved in a fixed avocation and course before he is capable of judging what is best for him. For as to what they say of the Hercules of Prodicus, as quoted by Xenophon,[1] that when he was just approaching maturity—the time given by nature to every one to choose what course of life he will enter—he went into a solitary place, and sitting there, hesitated long and seriously within himself, which of the two paths before him, one of pleasure, the other of virtue, it was better for him to take,—this might perchance happen to Hercules, the son of Jupiter, but not in like manner to us, who imitate whomsoever we see fit, and feel impelled toward their pursuits and modes of life, yet still oftener, imbued with the advice of our parents, are drawn into their manners and habits; while others, still, are carried away by popular opinion, and make choice of those things that seem most charming to the multitude. Yet some, whether by happy fortune, or by goodness of nature, or by parental discipline, enter upon the right way of living.

33. But the rarest description is of those who, endowed either with the prestige of surpassing genius, or with pre-eminent culture and

---

1. Xenophon, in the *Memorabilia*, gives this story by Prodicus, as cited by Socrates.

learning, or with both, have time to deliberate what course of life they would prefer to follow,—in which deliberation the issue should be made to conform to one's own natural bias. For while in the details of conduct we determine what is becoming from a man's native disposition, so in ordering the entire course of life much greater care should be taken that we may be consistent with ourselves so long as we live, and may not falter in the discharge of any one duty. But while in determining our course nature has the greatest influence, fortune comes next in controlling power, and account must be taken of both in choosing a mode of life,—yet most, of nature. For Nature is far the more stable and consistent of the two, so that Fortune—herself mortal—sometimes seems to be in conflict with Nature, the immortal. Let him, then, who refers his entire plan of life to his nature so far as it is unvitiated, go on as he has begun (for this is in the highest degree becoming), unless he be made aware that he was mistaken in his choice. If this take place (and it may), a change of habits and of plans is requisite. If circumstances favor this change, we can make it with a good measure of ease and convenience; otherwise, it must be made gradually and step by step, just as it is more becoming, in the opinion of the wise, to unknit gradually friendships which no longer please or satisfy us, than to cut[1] them in sunder with a single stroke. But when our mode of life is changed, we ought by all means to take heed that we present some show of sufficient reason. To return to what I said awhile ago as to the fitness of imitating parents and ancestors, an exception is to be made, in the first place, as to their faults, which we are not to reproduce; and, in the next place, if nature will not permit this imitation in certain particulars,—as the son of the elder Africanus[2] (who adopted the younger Africanus, the son of Paulus) on account of feeble health could not resemble his father as his father had resembled his grandfather,—if, for instance, one cannot frequent the courts as an advocate, or hold the ear of the people in their assemblies, or conduct military enterprises, he ought at least to

---

1. Latin, *dissuere—praecidere;* to unsew—to cut.

2. Publius Cornelius Scipio Africanus, bearing the same name with his father, the conqueror of Hannibal, whose father was Publius Cornelius Scipio, alternately victor and vanquished in the first Punic war. This second Africanus was regarded as superior in ability, no less than in learning and elegant culture, to all the other members of the Scipio *gens,* but was too feeble in health to take any part in public affairs, except in the peaceful offices of Augur and Flamen Dialis. He had no children, but adopted a son of Lucius Aemilius Paulus, Publius Cornelius Scipio Aemilianus Africanus, under whose generalship Carthage was finally subdued, and the city destroyed.

exhibit the qualities which are at his own command, justice, good faith, generosity, moderation, temperance, so that public opinion may not require of him those things in which he is inevitably deficient. But the best inheritance that fathers can give their children, more precious than any patrimony however large, is reputation for virtue and for worthy deeds, which if the child disgraces, his conduct should be branded as infamous and impious.

34. Since the same duties are not assigned to different periods of life, some belonging to the young, others to those more advanced in years, this distinction needs to be spoken of. It is, then, the part of the young man to revere his elders, and to choose from among them the best and the most approved, on whose advice and authority he may rely; for the inexperience of early life demands the wisdom of older men for its stability and its right direction. But most of all is this early age to be guarded against sensuality, and to be trained in labor and endurance, both of mind and of body, that the capacity of persistent diligence may be developed alike for military service and for civic duty. Moreover, when the young wish to relax their minds and to give themselves up to enjoyment, let them beware of excess, let them keep modesty in mind, which they will do the more if their elders will interest themselves also in matters of this sort. But for old men it would seem that bodily labor ought to be slackened, while mental efforts are to be even increased. At the same time they should take pains to aid their friends, and the young men, and, above all, the state, as much as possible by their counsel and experience. But nothing is to be more shunned by old age than self-surrender to listlessness and indolence. Luxurious living, too, unbecoming at any period of life, is most shameful for old age; and if to this licentiousness be added, the evil is double; for thus old age at once disgraces itself, and makes the excess of youth still more shameless.

Still further, it is not irrelevant to treat of the duties of magistrates and of those in private life, of citizens[1] and of foreigners. It is, then, the special function of the magistrate to regard himself as representing the person of the state, and bound to maintain its dignity and honor, to enforce the laws, to define conflicting rights, and to bear in mind whatever is committed to his good faith. The private citizen ought to live on fair and equal terms with his fellow-citizens, neither cringing

---

1. Latin, *privatorum—civium*, referring to the same persons, in contradistinction, first to magistrates, and secondly to foreigners.

and grovelling, nor yet assuming supercilious airs. Then too, in the
state he ought to choose those things which are peaceful and honorable;
for we are wont to feel and to say that such a man is a good citizen.
It is the duty of a foreigner and a temporary resident to do nothing
beyond his own business, not to pry into the concerns of other people,
and, least of all, to be meddlesome in the affairs of the state in which
he is an alien. Thus, for the most part, duties can be ascertained, when
the inquiry is raised what is becoming and what is fitting for different
persons, occasions, and ages. But there is nothing which is so becoming
as to maintain consistency in all that we do and undertake.

35. Since becomingness in all that is done and said has its place also
in the movement and attitude of the body, and consists in three things,
beauty, order, and attire fitted for the work in hand, difficult to express
in words,—but it will be enough if they are felt,—and since in these is
included our care to win the approval of those among whom we live,
a few things ought to be said as to these particulars. In the beginning
Nature seems to have made great account of our bodies, having placed
in plain sight our frame and such parts of our structure as have a
comely appearance, while she has covered and concealed those parts
of the body bestowed for the needs of nature, which might have an
unshapely and ugly aspect. This so careful construction of Nature the
modesty of men has followed; for the very things which Nature has
hidden all persons of sound mind keep out of sight, and are at pains
to obey the necessities connected with them as secretly as possible.
Moreover, as to these same parts of the body, whose uses are necessary,
they call neither them nor their uses by their proper names, and what
it is not disgraceful to do, if it be only in secret, it is obscene to name.
Thus the open doing of these things and the obscene mention of them
are equally liable to the charge of immodesty. Nor is any heed to be
given to the Cynics, or to those Stoics who are almost Cynics,[1] who
make it a matter of reproach and ridicule that we deem things that

---

1. The Cynics undoubtedly took their name from the κυνόσαργες,—one of the Athenian gymnasia in which their founder, Antisthenes, a pupil of Socrates, held his school; but some by no means contemptible authorities derive the name from κύων, *a dog*, and ascribe it to the snarling habit of the early disciples of the school, who were wont to sneer and scoff at what the rest of the world admired and prized. Diogenes of Sinope represented this type of character. Stoicism, in the person of Zeno, sprang out of the bosom of Cynicism, and embodied in its philosophy and ethics the fundamental principle of Antisthenes, that virtue is not the supreme, but the sole good. The later Cynics were characterized mainly by insolence, gratuitous indecency, and aimless asceticism.

are not shameful in fact unfit to be called by their right names, while we apply their proper names to things that are really shameful. Thus theft, fraud, and adultery are shameful in fact, but it is not obscene to call them by their names; while to perpetuate one's family is right in fact, yet obscene in name. On this notion those same philosophers hold prolix arguments at the expense of modesty. But let us follow Nature, and refrain from whatever lacks the approval of eye and ear. Let attitude, gait, mode of sitting, posture at table, countenance, eyes, movement of the hands, preserve the becomingness of which I speak. In these matters there are two extremes to be especially shunned,—on the one hand, effeminacy or daintiness, on the other, coarseness or rusticity. Nor ought it to be admitted that these rules, though proper for actors and public speakers, are matters of indifference to us. The custom of actors, from ancient tradition, carries modesty so far that no one is permitted to go upon the stage without drawers, in the fear that in case of the accidental exposure of certain parts of the body they may present an unbecoming spectacle. Our usage also forbids sons of ripe age from bathing with their fathers, sons-in-law with their fathers-in-law. This kind of modesty is to be adhered to, especially as Nature herself is mistress and guide.

36. While there are two kinds of beauty, in one of which grace, in the other dignity, predominates, we ought to regard grace as belonging to woman, dignity to man. Let then every species of apparel or adornment unworthy of a man be removed from his person, and let him guard against similar faults in attitude and gesture. For the manners of the wrestling ground[1] are apt to be somewhat disagreeable, and the affected attitudes of actors frequently give offence; while in the entire carriage of the body whatever is direct and simple receives commendation. Dignity of person is to be made sure by healthiness of complexion, and the complexion is to be maintained by bodily exercise. There should be rendered, with reference to neatness, a regard not offensively remiss, nor yet over-punctilious, just sufficient to avoid rustic and ill-bred slovenliness. The same rule is to be observed in dress, in which, as in most things, that which is becoming lies between the two extremes. Care must also be taken lest in our gait we accustom

---

1. *Palaestrici motus,* literally, palaestric movements. The *palaestra* was the resort of the young men of wealth and fashion, and thus a nursery of foppish manners no less than of bodily vigor.

ourselves to effeminate slowness, like the litters that carry in procession the images of the gods, or when time presses attempt excessive speed, in consequence of which panting ensues, the countenance is changed, the features are distorted, from all which the obvious inference is that there is a lack of stead-fastness in the character. But much greater pains should be taken lest the movements of the mind should transcend their natural equipoise; and this we shall effect if we guard against violent emotions and fits of despondency, and if we keep our minds intent on the observance of what is becoming. But the operations of the mind are of two kinds,—the one of thought, the other of impulse. Thought is occupied chiefly in seeking the truth; impulse urges to action. Care, then, is to be taken that we employ thought on the best subjects possible, and that we make impulse obedient to reason.

37. To pass to another subject, the power of speech being great, and of two kinds, the one of oratory, the other of conversation, let oratory find place in the arguments of courts, popular assemblies, and the Senate; let conversation have its scope in smaller circles, in the discussion of ordinary affairs, in the gatherings of friends,—let it also follow[1] convivial entertainments. The rhetoricians give rules for oratory; there are none for conversation. Yet I know not but that conversation might also have its rules. Masters are found when learners want them; but there are none who make conversation a study, while the rhetoricians have crowds of pupils. Yet the rules given about words and sentences apply to conversation no less than to oratory. And since we have the voice as the organ of speech, let us at least attempt two things as to the voice,—to have it distinct, and to have it pleasing to the ear. For both we must of course look to nature; but the one may be improved by practice, the other by imitating those who pronounce neither too broadly nor too rapidly. There was nothing in the Catuli[2] that would make you think them of exquisite taste in literature,—though they were men of letters, but only as others are,—yet they were thought to speak the Latin language as perfectly as it could be spoken. Their pronunciation was

---

1. *Sequatur*, which I have translated literally; for so far as I have been able to trace the festal habits of the ancients, from Homer's heroes downward, they ate in silence, and talked afterward. This is implied in the uses of the term συμπόσιον, *symposium*, a drinking together after the more solid portions of the feast have been disposed of.

2. Both of them men who held high places in the republic, and were worthy of its better days. The father was distinguished as an orator, and both father and son were among the foremost of their respective times in solid learning and in elegant culture.

sweet to the ear; the separate letters were neither drawled nor clipped, so as to avoid equally indistinctness and affectation; they spoke without effort, in a voice neither languid nor shrill. Lucius Crassus[1] had a more copious flow of language, with no less humor; yet the reputation of the Catuli as good talkers was fully equal to his. Caesar, the brother[2] of the elder Catulus, surpassed them all in wit and humor, so that when he spoke in the courts in his conversational way he was more efficient than other advocates with their set speeches. On all these matters we must bestow labor, if we aim at what is becoming in every detail of conduct.

Let then conversation, in which the followers of Socrates are pre-eminent, be easy, and by no means prolix; let politeness be always observed, nor must one debar others from their part, as if he had sole right to be heard; but, as in all things else, so in social intercourse, let him regard alternation as not unfair. Then, too, let him at the outset consider on what sort of subjects he is talking; if on serious things, let him show due gravity; on amusing, grace. Especially let him take heed lest his conversation betray some defect in his moral character, which is most frequently the case when the absent are expressly ridiculed or spoken of slanderously and malignly, with the purpose of injuring their reputation. For the most part, conversation relates to private affairs, or politics, or the theory and practice of the arts. Pains must then be taken that, if the conversation begins to wander off to other subjects, it be recalled to these. Yet reference must be had to the persons present; for we are not all interested in the same things, at all times, and in a similar degree. We should always observe, also, the length of time to which the pleasure of conversation extends, and as there was reason for beginning, so let there be a limit at which there shall be an ending.

38. But as it is a most fitting rule for the entire life, that we shun passion, by which I mean emotions that transcend the control of reason, so conversation ought to be free from emotions of this kind, that thus no anger or inordinate desire may show itself, and that at the same time there be no appearance of listlessness, or indifference, or anything of the kind. We must also take special care to preserve the bearing of respect and esteem for those with whom we converse. There is sometimes occasion for administering reproof, in which we must perhaps use a

---

1. The greatest orator of his age. He was in his prime in Cicero's boyhood.
2. They had the same mother; their fathers were of different *gentes*,—Catulus being of a plebeian, Caesar of a patrician *gens*.

greater stress of voice and a keener severity of diction; indeed, this may need to be carried so far as to make us seem under the influence of anger. But we shall have recourse to this kind of oral castigation, as to the cautery and the knife, rarely and reluctantly, nor ever, unless it be necessary in the absence of any other remedy. And at all events let anger be kept far away; for with anger nothing can be done rightly, nothing judiciously. But in most cases we can administer mild reproof, yet combined with earnestness, so that at once due severity may be employed and invective avoided. Moreover, the very bitterness which our reproof carries with it should be made to appear as designed for the benefit of the person reproved. It is right, also, even in our disputes with those the most hostile to us, and even though we receive from them unmerited reproach, to maintain a serious bearing indeed, but to exclude irritation. For what is done under some degree of excitement cannot be done with self-respect or with the approval of bystanders. Still further, it is in bad taste to talk about one's self, especially to lie about one's self, and with the derision of the audience to play the part of the Braggart Soldier.[1]

39. Since I want to make a thorough discussion of everything involving the question of duty,—for such is my purpose,—I ought to say also what sort of a house, in my opinion, should belong to a man in high office and conspicuous station. The ultimate end, of course, is convenience, and to this the plan of the building should be adapted, while at the same time care should be taken as regards stateliness of appearance and amplitude of accommodation. We are told that it redounded to the honor of Cneius Octavius, the first of his family that was made consul, that he had built a splendid house, one in all respects magnificent, on the Palatine Hill,[2] which, being seen by the people at large, was thought to have procured for the owner, belonging to a family that had before held no high office, the votes that raised him to the consulship. This house Scaurus demolished, and built where it stood an addition to his own house. And so the former of the two, first of his race, brought the consulship into his house; the latter, the

---

1. *Militem gloriosum. Miles Gloriosus* is the title of a comedy of Plautus, in which Pyrgopolineces, a military braggadocio, is the principal personage. The character was a favorite one with the Roman comedians and stage-lovers. Thraso, in Terence's *Eunuchus*, plays this part so well, as to have enriched the English language with the adjective *thrasonical*.

2. *In Palatio*,—the Palatium was the most fashionable quarter on the Palatine Hill.

son of a man of distinguished eminence and renown, bore home to his enlarged house on the same spot not only failure as a candidate for the consulship, but disgrace and disaster.[1] In truth, high standing in the community should be adorned by a house, not sought wholly from a house; nor should the owner be honored by the house, but the house by the owner. Moreover, as in matters of various kinds one must take account not of himself alone, but of others also, so in the house of a distinguished man, into which many guests are to be received, and a multitude of men of all kinds are to be admitted, care must be taken to have it roomy. Under other circumstances a very large house is apt to bring discredit to its owner if it have the air of loneliness, especially if under some former owner it used to be thronged. For it is offensive to have it said by those who pass by,—

> *"O ancient house! Ah, how unlike a lord*
> *Now lords it over thee!"*[2]

which in these times may be said about many a house. But special care should be taken, if you build yourself, not to go beyond reasonable limits in costliness and splendor. In such extravagance great mischief is done by mere example; for very many are anxious, especially in this direction, to follow the example of distinguished men. Thus who imitates the virtue of Lucius Lucullus, a man of the highest character? But how many have imitated the magnificence of his villas![3] Here there certainly is need of a limit, and of a return to a moderate standard. This same standard ought to be applied to the entire habit and style of living. But enough on this head.

In whatever we do there are three things to be endeavored. The first is that impulse be subservient to reason, than which there is no more fitting rule for the observance of duty. In the next place, we should

---

1. Marcus Aemilius Scaurus, son of the Scaurus named in § 22, when candidate for the consulship, was accused of extortion in the government of Sardinia, and though undoubtedly guilty, was defended by Cicero, and was acquitted, but failed of election. Two years afterward he was accused of bribery, condemned, and banished.

2. From an unknown poet.

3. Lucullus would have transmitted to coming time a great name as the conqueror of Mithridates, had he not become still more famous by magnificence, ostentation, and extravagance in his villas, gardens, fish-ponds, and entertainments. A single supper is said to have cost him a sum equivalent in silver to about ten thousand dollars, in value to at least five times as much. From him is derived the word *lucullite*, both French and English, denoting a devotee of luxury.

make ourselves acquainted with the magnitude of the object in hand, so that we may take upon ourselves neither more nor less care and labor than the case demands. The third rule is that the outlay for show and parade be brought within moderate limits; and those limits are best kept when we maintain the becomingness of which I have already spoken, and suffer ourselves not to go beyond it. Yet of these three the most excellent is that impulse should be subservient to reason.

40. In the next place, I am to speak of the order of our doings and the fit arrangement of time, which are comprehended in the science which the Greeks term εὐταξίαν, yet not in its sense of moderation (which involves the idea of measure or quantity), but in that sense of εὐταξία[1] which implies the observance of order in time and place. Yet in favor of our calling this moderation, we might cite the definition of the Stoics, who say that moderation is the art of putting in the right place whatever is done or said. Thus the import of order and that of collocation seem identical with it; for they define order to be the putting of things in fit and suitable places, and say that the fit time is the place of an action,—the fit time for an action, which we call occasion, being called in Greek εὐκαιρία.[2] Thus it is that moderation, which I interpret as I have said, comes to denote skill in determining the fitness of times for specific acts. But the same definition may be given of prudence, of which I treated in the earlier part of this essay.[3] Here, however, our subject is regularity, self-control, and virtues of that kind. What belongs peculiarly to prudence has been spoken of in its proper place; but of the class of virtues which has of late occupied our attention, it remains

---

1. This word is used by Xenophon in the sense of *order*; by Thucydides, in that of *moderation*.

2. *Opportuneness.*

3. This passage, as it treats of the definition of words, can hardly be understood without the use of the specific Latin words, both defining and defined. I therefore give here a more literal translation: "I am to speak of the order of our doings and the fit arrangement of time, which are comprehended in the science which the Greeks term εὐταξία,—not in that meaning of the word which we term *modestia* in which *modus* is implied, but in that sense which denotes the order of time and place. Yet in favor of our translating the word (εὐταξία) *modestia*, it may be said that the Stoics define *modestia* as the art of putting whatever is done or said in the right place. Thus *ordo* and *collocatio* seem to have the same import with it. For they define *ordo* as the putting of things in fit and suitable places; but they say that the fit time is the place of an action,—the fit time being called in Greek εὐκαιρία, in Latin, *occasio*. Thus it is that *modestia*, interpreted as I have said, comes to denote skill in determining the fitness of time for specific acts. But the same definition may be given of *prudentia*, of which I treated in the early part of this essay."

for me to speak of what may fall under the head of modesty and of regard for the approval of those among whom we live.

Such, then, should be the order applied to whatever we do, that, as in a coherent speech, so in the life, all things should be fitted to one another, and in harmony with one another. For it is disgraceful and exceedingly blameworthy, on a serious subject to introduce the kind of talk that belongs to a festive occasion, or any wanton strain of utterance. When Pericles had Sophocles for a colleague in military command, and they had met on their common official duty, and, a handsome boy happening to pass by, Sophocles said, "Oh, Pericles, what a beautiful boy!" Pericles very fittingly answered, "It becomes a commander, Sophocles, to have his eyes as abstinent[1] as his hands."[2] Yet had Sophocles said the same at a trial of skill among athletes, he would have incurred no just censure. So great is the significance of both place and time. Thus, if one who is going to plead a cause should, on a journey or in walking, be self-absorbed in meditation, or if at such a time he be wrapt in earnest thought on any other subject, he cannot be blamed; but if he present this appearance on a festive occasion, he would be regarded as ill-bred, because unmindful of the fitness of time. Such things, indeed, as are at a very great remove from propriety, like singing in the forum, or any other gross misconduct, are readily perceived, nor do they stand in special need of admonition and direction. But one should avoid with peculiar care offences that seem small, and cannot be appreciated by the many. As in stringed instruments or flutes an expert detects discord, however slight, so we should in our lives be on the watch for even the least discord, and all the more so, inasmuch as the harmony of actions is greater and better than that of musical notes.

41. Therefore, as in stringed instruments the ears of musicians detect the slightest falsity of tone, so shall we, if we are willing to be keen and careful observers of faults, often learn great things from small. From the glance of the eyes, from the expansion or contraction of the brows, from depression, from cheerfulness, from laughter, from the tone of the voice, from silence, from a higher or lower key of utterance, and other similar tokens, we may easily determine which of the greater things that they typify are fittingly done and which of them are at variance with duty and nature. Nor is it unsuitable in matters of this

---

1. From lust.
2. From bribes.

sort to judge of the character of our actions by looking at others, so that we may ourselves avoid whatever is unbecoming in them; for it is the case—I know not how—that we perceive any delinquency more readily in others than in ourselves. Therefore those pupils whose faults their masters mimic in order to cure them are most easily corrected. Nor yet is it out of place, before forming our judgment in doubtful cases, to consult men of superior natural intelligence or those who have become wise by experience, and to ask them what they think as to any matters in which the question of duty is involved. Indeed, most persons are wont to be drawn in nearly the direction in which their nature leads them, and we want to learn of men, not merely what they say, but what they think, and also why.[1] As painters, and sculptors, and poets, too, like to have their work pass under review by the people, that if any fault is found by a considerable number of persons it may be corrected, and as they earnestly inquire both of themselves and of others wherein the fault consists, so for us there are many things to be done and left undone, and changed and corrected by the opinion of others. Concerning things done by established custom or in order to obey the laws of the state, there are no rules to be given; for custom and law are themselves rules. Nor ought any one to be led into the error of supposing that, if Socrates or Aristippus[2] did or said anything contrary to custom and to legal usage, he may regard the like as lawful for himself. They obtained this liberty by superior and divine endowments. The entire system of the Cynics also is to be shunned; for it is opposed to modesty, without which there can be neither right nor honor. But we ought to respect and revere those whose life has been passed in the transaction of honorable and important affairs, who have a right feeling toward the state, and have rendered or are still rendering it service, no less than those in civil office or military command; to pay great deference to old age; to yield precedence to the magistrates; to make a distinction between citizens and foreigners, and in the case of

---

1. Which we may learn by consulting men of sound discretion and practical experience.

2. Aristippus maintained that the pleasure that lies nearest, whatever it be, is to be sought and enjoyed, and that man has no other end of being. The records that remain of his life give reason for believing that his personal morality was not so bad as his philosophy; yet he was luxurious in his habits, boasted of his freedom from moral restraints, and boasted also of his ability to forego without a sense of loss the indulgences which he had made habitual. He was a hearer, not to say a pupil, of Socrates, whose eccentricities were abnormal in the direction of a severer type of virtue.

foreigners, between those who come in a private and those who come in a public capacity. In short, not to treat of particulars, we ought to cherish, defend, preserve, the common harmony and fellowship of the whole human race.

42. Now as to the trades and modes of getting gain that are to be regarded as respectable,[1] and those that are to be deemed mean and vulgar, the general opinion is as follows: In the first place, those callings are held in disesteem that come into collision with the ill will of men, as that of taxgatherers, as that of usurers. The callings of hired laborers, and of all who are paid for their mere work and not for skill, are ungenteel[2] and vulgar; for their wages are given for menial service. Those who buy to sell again as soon as they can are to be accounted as vulgar; for they can make no profit except by a certain amount of falsehood, and nothing is meaner than falsehood. All mechanics are engaged in vulgar business; for a workshop can have nothing respectable about it. Least of all can we speak well of the trades that minister to sensual pleasures,—

"Fishmongers, butchers, cooks, poulterers, and fishermen,"

as Terence says. Add, if you please, to this list perfumers, ballet-dancers, and the whole tribe of dice-players. The professions which require greater skill and are of no small benefit to the community, such as medicine, architecture, the instruction of youth in liberal studies, are respectable for those whose rank they suit.[3] Commerce,[4] if on a small scale, is to be regarded as vulgar; but if large and rich, importing much from all quarters, and making extensive sales without fraud, it is not so very discreditable. Nay, it may justly claim the highest regard, if the merchant, satiated, or rather contented with his profits, instead of any longer leaving the sea for a port,[5] betakes himself from the port

---

1. *Liberales*, worthy of a free man.
2. *Illiberales*, unworthy of a free man.
3. For men of senatorial, or even equestrian rank, these employments, if practised for gain, were regarded as derogating from respectability.
4. The Romans in general, till near the last days of the republic, despised commerce, and though they depended for grain in great part on Sicily and remoter provinces, it was long before they brought grain in their own ships. In Cicero's time, however, it was the reproach of the equestrian order that many members of it, tired of genteel poverty, were enriching themselves by commerce; and Cicero, as a *parvenu* in the Senate, was weak enough to fall in with this foolish prejudice.
5. Merchants, engaged in traffic from port to port, owned and commanded the ships that carried their goods.

itself to an estate in the country. But of all means of acquiring gain nothing is better than agriculture, nothing more productive, nothing more pleasant, nothing more worthy of a man of liberal mind. Since I have said enough of this in my Cato Major, you will find there what belongs to the subject.

43. I think that I have sufficiently expounded the way in which specific duties are derived under the several divisions of the right. But as to the very things that are right there may be sometimes a question as to alternatives,[1] of two right things which is the more imperatively right,—a subject omitted by Panaetius. Since all that is right is deduced from four divisions of virtue, the first, knowledge; the second, social obligation; the third, elevation of mind; the fourth, moderation,—these must of necessity be often brought into comparison with one another in determining a specific duty.

In my opinion the duties derived from the relations of society have a closer adaptation to nature[2] than those which are derived from knowledge, as may be established by this argument,—that should such a life fall to the lot of a wise man that in the full abundance of all things and in entire leisure he could consider and contemplate within his own mind whatever is worth knowing, yet, were his solitude such that he could never see a human face, he would rather die. Then, too, the chief of all the virtues, that wisdom which the Greeks term σοφίαν[3] (for prudence, which the Greeks call φρόνησιν,[4] has another, narrower meaning, namely, the knowledge of things to be sought and shunned),—the wisdom which I have designated as chief of the virtues is the knowledge of things divine and human, which comprises the mutual fellowship and communion of gods and men. But if wisdom is the greatest of the virtues, as it undoubtedly is, it follows of necessity that the duty derived from this fellowship and communion is the greatest of duties. Moreover, the knowledge and contemplation of nature are somehow defective and imperfect, unless they lead to some result in action; and

---

1. Latin, *contentio et comparatio*,—stretching two objects side by side, and determining their comparative length. See § 17.

2. A Stoic idea. The Stoics derived all duty from nature,—the nature of things, the nature of man. They therefore made nature the sole test of duty, and (if I may so express what in less awkward phrase would be less clear) regarded the greater or less naturalness of a duty as the criterion of its relative importance.

3. Σοφία primarily meant *sagacity*, but is commonly employed to denote *wisdom* in its broadest sense.

4. Φρόνησις means *prudence*, in the sense of practical wisdom.

this appropriate action is best recognized in care for the well-being of mankind. The virtue from which it springs belongs, then, to the sodality of the human race, and is therefore to be preferred to knowledge. That this is so, every excellently good man shows and indicates in very deed. For who is there so deeply interested in penetrating and understanding the nature of things, that if, while he is handling and contemplating subjects most worthy of being understood, there is suddenly announced to him some danger and peril of his country in which he can render aid and succor, will not abandon and fling away his learned pursuits, even though he imagines that he can number the stars and find out the dimensions of the universe? And he would do the same thing in the business or in the peril of a father or a friend. It is thus seen that the duties of justice which concern the interests of our fellow-men, than which nothing ought to be more sacred to man, are to have precedence over the pursuits and duties of knowledge.

44. Now those whose pursuits and whose entire life have been devoted to the acquisition of knowledge, have nevertheless not withdrawn from the obligation of contributing to the advantage and benefit of mankind; for they have so instructed many as to make them better citizens and more useful to their respective states. Thus Lysis, the Pythagorean, taught Epaminondas of Thebes, and Plato was the preceptor of Dion of Syracuse, and many others have had numerous pupils. I myself, in whatever I have contributed to the well-being of the state (if I have indeed contributed anything), entered upon the public service well furnished in point of teachers and teaching. Nor is it only when these men are living and present that they instruct and teach those desirous of learning; but they follow up this same work even after death by the records of their knowledge and wisdom. For there is no topic omitted by them that could relate to laws, to morals, to the government of the state; so that they seem to have bestowed their leisure on our business.[1] Thus the very men who are devoted to the pursuit of learning and wisdom employ their intelligence and practical discretion chiefly for the benefit of mankind. Therefore it is better to speak fluently, if wisely, than to think, no matter with what acuteness of comprehension, if the power of expression be wanting; for thought begins and ends in itself, while fluent speech extends its benefit to those with whom we

---

1. *Otium*, leisure; *negotium* = *nec otium*, business,—a favorite play upon words with Cicero, which we have not the means of rendering into English.

are united in fellowship. Moreover, as swarms of bees are not gathered for the purpose of making honeycombs, but make honeycombs because they are gregarious by nature, so, and even much more, men, sociable by nature, bring to their union skill in joint and associate action. Therefore, unless the virtue which consists in caring for the well-being of men, that is, in the maintenance of human society, accompany the knowledge of things, that knowledge must seem isolated and meagre; and equally loftiness of mind, if divorced from human society and fellowship, becomes mere brutality and savageness. Thus it is that the society and fellowship of men transcend in importance the pursuit of knowledge. Nor is it true, as some say, that it is on account of the necessities of life—because we could not obtain and accomplish what nature demands without the aid of others—that fellowship and society were initiated among men, but that if everything appertaining to subsistence and comfortable living were supplied for us, so to speak, as by a magic wand, every person of excelling genius, giving up all other concerns, would occupy himself wholly in knowledge and science. It is not so; for man in that case would shun solitude, and seek companionship in his pursuits,—would want now to teach, then to learn; now to hear, then to speak. Therefore every form of duty which is of avail for the union of men and the defence of society is to be regarded as of higher obligation than the duty which is dependent on abstract study and science.

45. It may perchance be asked whether this human fellowship which is most closely allied to nature is also always to have the precedence over modesty and decency. I think not. For there are certain things, some so repulsive, some so scandalous, that a wise man would not do them even to save his country. Posidonius[1] has brought together a great many of these things, some of them so foul, so indecent, that it would be offensive even to name them. These things, then, one will not do for the sake of the state, nor yet will the state demand that they should be done for its sake. But the question is the more easily settled, inasmuch as there cannot come any crisis in which it can be for the interest of the state that a wise man should do any of these things.

This, then, may be regarded as settled, that in choosing between

---

1. Posidonius was a Stoic, a disciple of Panaetius, a voluminous writer on an encyclopedic range of subjects. Of his works only fragments are preserved, and happily the catalogue of things not fit to be done has left no traces of itself. His works are known chiefly by copious extracts made by Athenaeus.

conflicting duties preference must be given to the class of duties essential to the maintenance of human society. Moreover, considerate action is the result of knowledge and prudence. It therefore follows that to act considerately is of more worth than to think wisely.[1] But I have said enough on this point; for this division of the subject has been so laid open that it cannot be difficult in an inquiry as to duty to see in any particular case which duty is to be regarded as of prime and which of secondary obligation.

But in society itself there are gradations of duties, from which it may be determined what one owes in any individual relation. Thus we are bound in obligation, first to the immortal gods, secondly to our country, thirdly to our parents, then by successive degrees to other persons more or less nearly related to us.

From this brief discussion light may be thrown, not only on the question whether certain specific acts are right or wrong, but also, when the choice lies between two right things, on the question which of the two is of the highest obligation. This last head, as I said above, is omitted by Panaetius. Let us go on now to what remains of the subject.

---

1. An inference so illogical as to seem an oversight.

Book II

1. I think, my son Marcus, that it has been sufficiently explained in my first book how duties are to be derived from the right, and from each of the four virtues which I named as divisions of the right. It comes next in order, to treat of those kinds of duties that belong to the adornment of life and the command of its utilities, to influence and resources of every description. Under this head I have said that the inquiry is, first, what is expedient and what inexpedient, and then, of expedient things which is the more expedient, which the most expedient. I shall proceed to the discussion of these things, after saying a few words concerning my design and method in writing on philosophical subjects.

Although, indeed, my books have roused not a few to the desire not only of reading, but of writing, still I sometimes fear that the mere name of philosophy may be offensive to certain worthy men, and that they may marvel that I spend so much labor and time upon it. In truth, so long as the state was administered by men of its own choice, I bestowed upon it all my care and thought. But when all things were held under the absolute sway of one man, and there was no longer room for advice or influence, while at the same time I had lost my associates in the guardianship of the state, men of the highest eminence, I did not abandon myself to melancholy, which would have consumed me had I not resisted it, nor yet, on the other hand, to sensual pleasures unworthy of a philosopher. And oh that the state had continued in the condition in which it recommenced its life,[1] and had not fallen into the hands of men desirous not so much of reforming as of revolutionizing its constitution! In that case, in the first place, as I used to do when the state stood on a firm basis, I should expend more labor in pleading than in writing; and in the next place, I should commit to writing not

---

1. After the assassination of Caesar, when for a very little while there seemed some hope of a return to republican institutions in fact as well as in name.

the subjects now in hand, but my arguments before the courts, as I have often done. But when the state, on which all my care, thought, labor, used to be expended, had utterly ceased to be, my forensic and senatorial literature was of course silenced. Yet since my mind could not be unemployed, having been conversant with these studies from my early days, I thought that my chagrin could be most honorably laid aside if I betook myself to philosophy, to which I devoted a large part of my youth as a learner, while after I began to hold important offices and gave myself wholly to the service of the state, philosophy had as much of my time as was not taken up by the claims of my friends and the public. Yet this time was all consumed in reading; I had no leisure for writing.

2. I seem, then, in the severest calamities to have attained at least this good fortune, that I am able to commit to writing subjects not sufficiently familiar to my fellow-countrymen, and yet preeminently worthy of their cognizance. For what, in the name of the gods, is more desirable than wisdom? What more to be prized? What better? What more worthy of man? It is the seekers of this, then, who are called philosophers; nor is philosophy, if you undertake to translate it, anything else than the love of wisdom. But wisdom, as defined by the ancients, is the knowledge of things divine and human, and of the causes by which these things are kept in harmony. I cannot well understand what he who blames the pursuit of this knowledge can regard as commendable. For if gratification of the mind and repose from care be sought, what pleasure can be compared with the pursuits of those who are always searching out what may look and tend toward a good and happy life? Or if regard is paid to consistency of character and to virtue, either this is the science[1] by which we may attain them, or there is none at all. To say that there is no science of these greatest of human interests when there are none of the smallest concerns that have not their science, is the language of men who talk without thinking, and who deceive themselves in matters of the highest moment. Then, too, if there is any instruction in virtue, where should it be sought, when you turn away from this department of learning? But these things are usually discussed with greater precision in urging readers to the study of philosophy, as I have done in another treatise.[2] My present purpose

---

1. Latin, *ars;* but *art* is here an inadequate rendering.
2. In *Hortensius.*

was simply to say why, deprived of opportunities for the service of the state, I chose this department of study above all others.

It is objected to me, and that too by educated and learned men, that I seem not to act consistently, when I say that nothing can be known with certainty, and yet am accustomed to give my opinion on other subjects, and am now setting forth the rules of duty. I could wish that these persons had an adequate understanding of my philosophical doctrine.[1] For I am not one of those whose minds drift about in uncertainty, and never have any definite aim. Indeed, what sort of an intellect, or rather of a life, would remain, if fixed principles not only of reasoning, but of conduct, were abolished? This is not my case; but while others say that some things are certain, some doubtful, so I, differing from them, call some things probable, some improbable. What is there, then, that can hinder me from pursuing those things that seem to me probable, rejecting those things that seem improbable, and, while I shun the arrogance of positive assertion, escaping the recklessness which is at the farthest remove from wisdom? All opinions are controverted by our school, on the ground that this very probability cannot be brought to light unless by a comparison of the arguments on both sides. These things, however, are, as I think, expounded with sufficient care in my Academics. But though you, my Cicero, are becoming versed in the most ancient[2] and noble of philosophies, under the guidance of Cratippus, who bears the closest resemblance to the illustrious founders of the school, I am unwilling that these speculations of mine, nearly allied to those of your school, should be unknown to you. But let us now take up the plan proposed for our discussion.

3. At the outset I proposed for the full discussion of duty five divisions, two relating to what is becoming and right; two to the conveniences of life, resources, influence, wealth; the fifth to the determination of our choice, whenever the right and the expedient might seem mutually repugnant. The divisions relating to the right, which I would have you thoroughly understand, are finished. This of which I am now going to treat is what is termed expediency, with reference to which custom has turned out of the right way, and has been gradually

---

1. That of the New Academy.
2. Cratippus was a Peripatetic, and thus regarded Aristotle as his master; but as Aristotle derived much of his philosophy from Plato, and Plato, much or all of his from Socrates, Cicero, with more rhetorical aptness than literal truth, antedates the school of which his son was the pupil.

brought to the point of separating the right from the expedient, and of maintaining that what is not expedient may be right, and what is not right, expedient, than which there could be no doctrine more pernicious to human well-being. There are, indeed, philosophers of the very highest authority who on strict and tenable grounds make a distinction in theory between three several kinds of excellence, which yet, as they admit, are inseparable in their nature; for whatever is just they regard as expedient, and likewise what is right as just. Hence it follows that whatever is right is also expedient.[1] Those who imagine that the distinction is not in mere theory, but in fact, often admiring adroit and crafty men, take roguery for wisdom. Their mistake ought to be eliminated, and the universal opinion brought over to the hope that men may learn to expect the attainment of what they desire by right purposes and honest deeds, not by fraud and roguery.

The means of sustaining human life are in part inanimate, as gold, silver, the products of the earth, and other things of that sort; in part, living beings that have their own instincts and appetites. Of these last some are destitute of reason, others are rational. Those destitute of reason are horses, oxen, other cattle, bees, by whose labor contribution is made to the service and subsistence of men. Of the rational there are named two classes,—the one of gods, the other of men. Reverence and purity will make the gods propitious. But next to and close after the gods, men can be of the greatest service to men. The same division applies to those things that cause injury and obstruction. But because it is thought that the gods do no injury, these being out of the question, men are regarded as most of all interfering injuriously with men.

Indeed, the very things that I have called inanimate are produced for the most part by the labor of men, nor could we have them unless handicraft and skill had given their aid, nor could we utilize them except under the management of men. Nor without the labor of man could there be any care of health, or cultivation of the soil, or harvesting and preservation of grain and other products of the ground. Nor could there be the exportation of our superfluous commodities, nor the importation of those in which we are lacking, unless men performed these offices. By parity of reason the stones that we need for our use could not be quarried from the earth,

---

1. A syllogism in *Barbara*.

"Nor iron, brass, silver, gold, be dug from their deep caverns,"[1]

without the labor and handicraft of men.

4. Whence, indeed, could houses, to dispel the severity of the cold and to allay the discomfort of the heat, have been furnished for mankind in the beginning, or how could they have been repaired, when made ruinous by storm, or earthquake, or age, unless society had learned to seek aid in these things from men? Take into the account also aqueducts, canals, works for the irrigation of fields, breakwaters, artificial harbors. Whence could we have these without the labor of men? From these and many other things it is obvious that we could in no wise have received the revenues and uses derived from inanimate objects without the skill and labor of men. Then, again, what revenue or what convenience could be derived from beasts, unless by the aid of men? For it was men certainly who were foremost in discovering what use we might make of the several beasts in our service; nor could we now without the labor of men either feed them, or tame them, or keep them, or receive returns from them in their season.[2] By men also those beasts that do harm are killed, and those that can be of use are captured. Why should I enumerate the multitude of arts without which life could not have been at all? How would the sick be cured, what would be the enjoyment of the healthy, what would be our food or our mode of living, did not so many arts give us their ministries? It is by these things that the civilized life of men is so far removed from the subsistence and mode of living of the beasts. Cities, too, could not have been built and peopled but for the association of men, in consequence of which laws and rules of moral conduct have been established, as also an equitable distribution of rights, and a systematic training for the work of life. These things have been followed by mildness of disposition and by modesty, and the consequence is that human life is better furnished with what it needs, and that by giving, receiving, and interchanging commodities and conveniences we may have all our wants supplied.

5. I am dwelling on this subject longer than is necessary; for who is there to whom what Panaetius says with no little prolixity is not perfectly obvious, that no one, either as a military commander or as a civil magistrate, could ever have carried into effect important and

---

1. A verse from some lost poem, probably the *Prometheus* of Attius.
2. For instance, wool, at the proper time of shearing.

serviceable measures without the zealous co-operation of men? He
names Themistocles, Pericles, Cyrus, Agesilaus, Alexander, who, he
says, could not have accomplished such great things without the aid of
men. He cites witnesses that are unnecessary in a matter beyond doubt.

Still further, as we obtain great benefits by the sympathy and co-
operation of men, so there is no degree of evil, however execrable,
which may not spring from man for man. There is extant a book about
the destruction of men,[1] by Dicaearchus, a distinguished and eloquent
Peripatetic, who, after enumerating other causes,—such as inunda-
tion, pestilence, perils of the desert, the sudden inrush of destructive
beasts[2] (by whose assaults, he says, whole races of men have been
consumed),—then shows by comparison how many more men have
been exterminated by the violence of men, that is, by wars or seditions,
than by all other forms of calamity.

Since, then, there is no doubt on this point, that men transcend all
other causes both of benefit and of injury to men, I maintain that it
is a special property of virtue to conciliate the minds of men, and to
make them availing for its own uses. Thus, while whatever in inanimate
objects and in the use and management of beasts redounds to human
benefit is to be ascribed to the mechanic arts, the good will of men,
prompt and ready for the improvement of our condition, is elicited only
by the wisdom and virtue which belong to men of superior excellence.

Indeed, all virtue may be said to consist in three things,[3] one of which
lies in the clear discernment of what is true and real in every subject,
of the correspondences of things, of their consequences, sources, and
causes; the second, in the restraining of those troubled movements of

---

1. This work has entirely perished. Dicaearchus, a contemporary and follower of
Aristotle, was a copious writer in the departments of geography and history, as well as of
philosophy. One of his books on "The Life of Greece," if we may judge by the fragments
of it that remain, would have been worth more than all other extant records of Athenian
life in his age.

2. I do not know that there is any ancient record of the extensive destruction of human
life by wild beasts, except that in the Old Testament (2 Kings xvii. 25), of the slaughter
of people by lions in some of the Samaritan cities. But there are several traditions of
instances in which the inhabitants of cities or towns were compelled to change their
abodes, and hardly without some loss of life, by devastating, tormenting, or perilous
incursions of mice, frogs, scorpions, serpents, moles, rabbits, and locusts.

3. We have here the first, fourth, and second of the cardinal virtues portrayed in Book
I. The third is omitted, as peculiarly non-utilitarian; the second has the third place, as
a text to be enlarged upon,—as the prime means of securing such utilities as men can
bestow.

mind which the Greeks call πάθη,[1] and in making the impulses which
they call ὁρμάς[2] obedient to reason; the third, in the considerate and
wise treatment of those with whom we are associated, by whose good
will we may have in full and overflowing measure whatever nature
craves, and by whose agency we may ward off impending evil, may
exact retribution of those who attempt to do us harm, and visit them
with such punishment as justice and humanity will permit.

6. By what means we can attain this capacity of winning and holding
men's affections, I will shortly expound; but there are a few things to be
said first. Who does not know that Fortune has great power on either
side, whether toward prosperous or adverse events? For when we sail
under her propitious breath, we reach our desired port, and when she
sends a contrary wind, we founder. Fortune herself, then, occasions
some calamities—though comparatively rare—independently of human agency: in the first place, from inanimate things, as by gales, tem-
pests, shipwrecks, falling buildings, conflagrations; then from beasts,
by stings, bites, assaults. These, as I have said, are comparatively infre-
quent. But the destruction of armies, as of three very recently,[3] and of
many others in former times; the murder of commanders, as lately that
of an eminent and remarkable man;[4] the enmity, also, of the multitude,
and by its means the exile,[5] ruin, flight, often of well-deserving citizens; and, on the other hand, prosperous events, civic honors, military
commands, victories,—these, although they are partly dependent on
fortune, cannot be brought to pass on either side without the aid and
endeavor of men. This, then, being understood, I am to explain how we
can elicit and call forth the good will of men for our own benefit. If the
discussion shall seem too long, let it be compared with the advantage
to be derived from it. It will then, perhaps, seem too brief.

Whatever, then, men bestow upon a man to enrich and ennoble him,
they do it, either from kind feeling to a person whom for some reason
they hold dear; or from respect for one to whose virtue they look up,
and whom they think worthy of as ample good fortune as can accrue
to him; or for one in whom they have confidence, and whose counsel

1. Passions.
2. Impulses.
3. The army of Pompey the Great, in Pharsalia; that of his son, at Munda; and that of
Scipio, at Thapsus,—all defeated by Julius Caesar.
4. The murder of Pompey the Great, in Egypt.
5. Cicero undoubtedly has in mind, here, his own exile by the machinations of Clodius.

and aid for their own benefit they hope in return; or for one whom they hold in dread for his capacity to injure them; or, on the other hand, for those from whom they have expectations, as when kings and demagogues distribute largesses; or, finally, when they are moved by price and bribe, which is the meanest and vilest way, both for those whose favor is held by it and for those who endeavor to resort to it; for it is a bad case when what ought to be effected by virtue is attempted by money. Yet since subsidies of this kind are sometimes necessary,[1] I will define their proper use, when I shall have first spoken of things which bear a closer relation to virtue. Moreover, men put themselves under the command and power of others for several reasons. They are led to this either by kind feeling, or by the greatness of favors received, or by the high social position of him to whom they yield deference, or by hope that such a course will be of use to them, or by fear of being forcibly compelled to render obedience; or they are attracted by the prospect of generous gifts and by promises; or, lastly, as we often see in our state, they are hired for wages.

7. But of all things nothing tends so much to the guarding and keeping of resources as to be the object of affection; nor is anything more foreign to that end than to be the object of fear. Ennius says most fittingly:—

"Hate follows fear; and plotted ruin, hate."

It has been lately demonstrated, if it was before unknown, that no resources can resist the hatred of a numerous body. It is not merely the destruction of this tyrant, whom the state, subdued by armed force, endured so long as he lived and obeys most implicitly now that he is dead,[2] that shows how far the hatred of men may prove fatal; but similar deaths of other tyrants, hardly one of whom has escaped a like fate, teach this lesson. For fear is but a poor guardian for permanent possession, and, on the other hand, good will is faithful so long as there can be need of its loyalty. Those who hold under their command subjects forcibly kept down must indeed resort to severity, as masters toward their slaves when they cannot otherwise be restrained. But

---

1. Cicero here refers, not to bribery, but to such liberal uses of money as he designates with approval in the sequel.

2. The Senate were induced by Antony to pass sundry laws, the drafts of which he professed—in part, no doubt, falsely—to have found among Caesar's papers.

nothing can be more mad than the policy of those who in a free state conduct themselves in such a way as to be feared. For though the laws be submerged by some one man's power, though liberty be panic-stricken, yet in time they rise to the surface, either by opinions circulated, though unuttered, or by the quiet mustering of votes that shall dispose of the high offices of state. Men indeed feel more keenly the suppression of liberty than any evils incident to its preservation. Let us then embrace the policy which has the widest scope, and is most conducive, not to safety alone, but to affluence and power, namely, that by which fear may be suppressed, love retained. Thus shall we most easily obtain what we desire both in private and in public life. For it is inevitable that those who wish to be feared should themselves fear the very persons by whom they are feared. What, for instance, must have been the case with the elder Dionysius?[1] With what tormenting fear must he have been racked, when, dreading the barber's razor, he used to singe off his own beard with burning coals? What are we to think of Alexander of Pherae?[2] In what state of mind must we suppose him to have lived, who, as we read the record, though somewhat fond of his wife Thebe, yet when he came from supper to her chamber, ordered a barbarian attendant, and indeed one, as we are told, branded with the marks of a Thracian,[3] to precede him with a drawn sword, and sent in advance some of his body-guards to search the woman's boxes, and see whether there were not some weapon concealed among the clothes? O wretch, to think a tattooed savage more to be trusted than his own wife! Yet he was in the right; for he was slain by that very wife,[4] because she suspected him of adultery. Nor indeed is there any ruling power strong

---

1. Of Syracuse,—a sovereign of signal ability, energy, magnificence, and public spirit, a liberal patron of literature and philosophy, but at the same time jealous, suspicious, arbitrary, and cruel,—leaving at once vestiges of true greatness as a king, and records, undoubtedly in large part authentic, of acts that disgrace humanity. The story is that while his daughters were very young, he made them shave him and cut his hair; when they were old enough for him to fear them, he used shoots of the walnut (*juglans*) to burn off his beard. He had a ditch round his bed, with a drawbridge commanded by himself.

2. He came to the throne by the murder of his uncle and predecessor.

3. The Thracians, who were accounted as barbarians, were employed as body-guards by some of the petty tyrants of the Grecian cities, as the Swiss have been employed in Paris and in Rome, and as Scythians were employed in a similar capacity at Athens.

4. Alexander's chamber was at the top of a ladder, and a fierce dog was chained at the door. His wife concealed her three brothers in the house during the day, removed the dog after Alexander was asleep, covered the steps of the ladder with wool, and led the young men up to murder her husband.

enough to be enduring, when it makes itself the object of dread. Of
this we may find an example in Phalaris[1] whose cruelty was notorious
beyond that of any other tyrant, who perished, not by treachery, like
that Alexander of whom I have just spoken,—not by the hands of a
few, like this tyrant of ours, but who was assailed by the whole mass
of the people of Agrigentum. What? Did not the Macedonians desert
Demetrius,[2] and in a body betake themselves to Pyrrhus? What? When
the Lacedaemonians usurped power that was not rightfully theirs,
did not almost all their allies leave them, and show themselves idle
spectators of the disaster at Leuctra?[3]

8. I prefer on such a subject to draw my examples from foreign states
rather than from our own. Yet so long as the sway of the Roman people
was maintained by the bestowal of benefits, not by injustice, wars were
waged either in defence of our allies or of our own government; the
issues of our successful wars were either merciful or no more severe
than necessity demanded; our Senate was the harbor and refuge of
kings, tribes, nations; while our magistrates and military commanders
sought to obtain the highest praise from this one thing,—the guarding
of the interests of our provinces and our allies by equity and good faith.
Our sovereignty might then have been termed the patronage, rather
than the government, of the world. We previously had encroached
by degrees on this habit and policy; after Sulla's victory we entirely
departed from it; for nothing any longer appeared inequitable toward
our allies, after so much cruelty had been exercised upon our own
citizens. In his case a worthy cause[4] was crowned by a disgraceful

---

1. Phalaris is almost a mythical personage. Different authorities assign dates nearly a
century apart for the beginning of his reign, the latest date being 570 b. c. There are also
opposite traditions as to his character, some authorities representing him as mild and
humane.

2. Demetrius Poliorcetes. Pyrrhus, King of Epeirus, had invaded Macedonia, and
when Demetrius marched to meet him, the Macedonian army *en masse* passed over to
the invader. Demetrius was a ruler of marvellous vigor, and though sometimes truculent
and cruel, and always grossly sensual, was not wholly devoid of humane and generous
feeling.

3. The campaign against Thebes, closed by the battle of Leuctra, was opposed to the
wishes of all the allies of Sparta, and their soldiers were accused by the Spartans of utter
inefficiency in the field, to be accounted for only by their reluctance to engage in the
conflict.

4. Sulla was the champion of the aristocracy, and thus far his position had Cicero's
approval and sympathy.

victory; for he dared to say, when under the auctioneer's spear[1] he sold
in the market-place the property of good men and rich men who were
undoubtedly citizens, that he was selling his booty. He was succeeded
by one who in an impious cause, after even a more disgraceful victory,
not merely offered for public sale the goods of individual citizens,
but embraced whole provinces and countries in one destructive ban.
And so, foreign nations being thus oppressed and ruined, in token of
our forfeited empire, we saw Massilia borne in effigy in a triumphal
procession, and a triumph celebrated over that city without whose aid
our commanders never gained a Transalpine triumph.[2] I might mention
many other abominable things done to our allies, if the sun had ever
beheld anything more shameful than this very transaction. We therefore
are justly punished; for unless we had so often had impunity from guilt,
so great liberty of sinning would never have come into the hands of
one man, whose heritage of property falls to few, that of depraved
desire to many bad men. Nor indeed will there ever be wanting seed
and pretext for civil wars, so long as abandoned men remember and
hope to see again that bloody spear which Publius Sulla[3] brandished
in the dictatorship of his kinsman, not refusing to be salesman under a
more atrociously guilty spear thirty-six years afterward; while another
Sulla,[4] who in the former dictatorship was secretary, in this last was
city-quaestor. Hence it ought to be inferred that while such prizes
are held in view, civil wars will never cease to be. And so only the
walls of the city stand and remain, and even they already fear the
extremity of crime; the state itself we have utterly lost. Moreover (for I
must return to the point under discussion), we have fallen into these
calamities because we preferred to be feared rather than to be loved
and esteemed. If these things could befall the Roman people exercising

---

1. A spear stuck in the ground was in Rome, as a red flag is with us, the sign of a sale
at auction.

2. Massilia (*Marseilles*), a city settled by Grecian colonists, and in Caesar's time second
to no other city in the world as a seat of extensive commerce, was from the first a faithful
ally of Rome, and, when the region of Gaul in which it is situated became a Roman
province, that city was suffered to retain its independence. In the civil war the Massilians
espoused the cause of Pompey, and shut their gates against Caesar, who besieged and
took the city, and had a model of it borne in procession in his triumph.

3. Publius Cornelius Sulla, the nephew of the dictator, and, about midway between his
dictatorship and Caesar's, found guilty of bribery when a candidate for the consulship.

4. Cornelius Sulla, a freedman of the dictator, who, as Sulla's secretary, could secure
large profits from confiscated property, and as quaestor under Caesar had access to the
city treasury.

an unrighteous sway, what ought individuals to think as to their own conduct and fortune? Since it is manifest that the power of good will is great, that of fear feeble, it follows that we should inquire by what means we can most easily obtain, together with respect and confidence, that love of others which we crave. We do not all, indeed, need this love in an equal degree; for it must be determined by each person's plan of life, whether he requires the love of many, or whether it is enough for him to be held in dear regard by a few. This, however, may be accounted as certain, that it is a prime and most essential requisite, to have the enduring intimacy of friends who love us and hold us in high esteem. This one thing, precious above all others, if attained, leaves but little difference between persons of the loftiest rank and those in moderate condition, and it is almost equally attainable by those of either class. All, perhaps, do not alike need promotion, and fame, and the good will of the citizens at large; but yet, if one has these, they render some help, as to other ends, so to the obtaining of friendships.

9. But I have treated of friendship in another book, under the title of Laelius. Let me now speak of fame. Though on that subject also I have written two books,[1] let me touch briefly upon it here, since it is of the utmost service in the administration of important affairs.

The highest fame, and that to which there are no drawbacks, consists of these three things,—the affection of the multitude, their confidence, and their regarding a person as worthy of honor because they hold him in admiration.[2] Moreover, these requisites to fame—to speak plainly and concisely—are obtained from the multitude by nearly the same means by which they are obtained from individuals. But there is also a certain other avenue to the popular favor, by which we may, as it were, steal into the affections of all.

Of the three things just named, let us consider, first, the rules for winning good will. It is, indeed, best secured by conferring benefits. But, in the second place, favor is elicited by the will to do good, even if the means of beneficence chance to be insufficient. The love of the multitude, indeed, is strongly excited by the very report and reputation of liberality, beneficence, honesty, good faith, and all those virtues

---

1. They are both lost. Cicero mentions one of them in *Letters to Atticus*, xvi. 27. "Librum tibi celerrime mittam de gloria."

2. This is evidently meant to exclude the meaner ways by which men insinuate themselves into popular favor.

which are included in gentleness of manners and affability. For since that very style of character which we call right and becoming, in itself, gives us pleasure, and by its nature and aspect captivates the minds of all, and shines forth with the greatest lustre from the virtues that I have named, we are therefore compelled by Nature herself to love the persons in whom we think that these virtues are found. These, however, are only the most efficient causes of good will; for there may be some others, though of less weight.

Of the confidence which may be reposed in us there are two efficient causes, our having a reputation for discretion and, at the same time, for honesty. For we have confidence in those whom we think our superiors in intelligence, who, as we believe, look into the future, and who, when an affair is in agitation and a crisis is reached, can clear it of difficulty, and take counsel according to circumstances (for this men regard as true and serviceable discretion); while the confidence reposed in honest and faithful men, that is, in good men, is such that there can rest upon them no suspicion of fraud and wrong. And so we think that our personal security, our fortunes, our children, can be most fittingly intrusted to their care. Of these two qualities, then, honesty has the greater power to create confidence; for while without discretion honesty has sufficient prestige, discretion without honesty can be of no avail in inspiring confidence. For the more skilful and adroit one is, for this very reason is he the more odious and the more open to suspicion, if he has no reputation for honesty. Intelligence, then, combined with honesty, will have all the power that it can desire in creating confidence; honesty without discretion will have much influence toward that end; discretion without honesty will be of no avail whatever.

10. But if any one may have wondered, why, while all philosophers alike maintain, and I myself have often asserted, that whoever has one virtue has all, I now separate them as if a man could be honest without being wise also, my answer is that the nicety of expression employed when the inmost truth is under discussion is one thing; the language used when what we say is entirely adapted to popular opinion is another. Therefore, on this head I am speaking as people in general do, when I call some men brave, others good, others wise; for I ought to employ common and usual terms when I am speaking of public opinion, and Panaetius employed them in the same way. But let us return to our subject.

Of the three requisites for fame, the third that I named was this,—
that men should so hold us in admiration as to regard us worthy of
honor. Men generally admire all things that they see to be great and
beyond their expectation, and specially in individual objects such un-
expected good qualities as they discern. Therefore they admire and
extol with the highest praise those men in whom they think that they
perceive certain rare and surpassing virtues; while they look down with
contempt on those in whom they imagine that there is no manliness,
no spirit, no energy. For they do not despise all of whom they think
ill. They do not despise, indeed, those whom they regard as villainous,
malicious, fraudulent, capable of doing mischief,—by no means; of
persons of this sort they think ill. But, as I have said, those are despised
who, as the saying is, are of no good to themselves or to any one else,
in whom there is no work, no industry, no forethought. On the other
hand, those are regarded with a certain measure of admiration, who
are thought to excel others in virtue, and to be free not only from all
disgrace, but also from those vices which their fellow-men cannot easily
resist. For sensual pleasures, the most alluring of mistresses, turn away
the minds of the greater part of mankind from virtue, and equally when
the fiery trial of affliction[1] comes most persons are beyond measure
terrified. Life, death, riches, poverty, most violently agitate the great
mass of mankind. When men with a lofty and large soul look down
on these experiences, whether prosperous or adverse, while any great
and honorable object of endeavor proposed to them converges and
concentrates their whole being in its pursuit, who can fail to admire
in them the splendor and beauty of virtue?

11. This contempt of the mind for outward fortunes thus excites great
admiration; and most of all, justice, for which one virtue men are called
good, seems to the multitude a quality of marvellous excellence,—and
not without good reason; for no one can be just, who dreads death,
pain, exile, or poverty, or who prefers their opposites to honesty. Men
have, especially, the highest admiration for one who is not influenced
by money; for they think that the man in whom this trait is made
thoroughly manifest has been tested by fire.

Thus justice constitutes all three of the requisites to fame which
I have named,—affection, because it aims to do good to the greatest
number, and for the same reason, confidence and admiration, because

---

1. Latin, *dolorum faces*,—the torches, or cautery, of sorrows.

it spurns and neglects those things to which most men are drawn with burning greediness. Moreover, in my opinion, every mode and plan of life demands the aid of men, and craves especially those with whom there may be friendly conversational intercourse, which is not easy, unless you are looked upon as a good man. Therefore, even to a recluse, or to one who passes his life in the country, the reputation of honesty is essential, and the more so because, if he do not have it, in his defenceless condition, he will be assailed by many wrongs. Those, too, who sell and buy, hire and lease, and are involved in business affairs, need honesty for the management of their concerns. The force of this virtue is such that those who obtain their subsistence by crime and guilt cannot live entirely without honesty. For he who takes anything by stealth or force from a fellow-robber cannot maintain his place in a band of robbers; and even the man who is called captain of a crew of pirates, if he were not impartial in the division of their plunder, would be either killed or deserted by his crew. Indeed, it is said that even among robbers there are laws which they obey, which they hold sacred. Thus by fairness in the distribution of booty, Bardylis, an Illyrian robber, of whom Theopompus makes mention, obtained great wealth, and Viriathus, the Lusitanian,[1] much greater, to whom indeed some of our armies and commanders gave way in battle, whom Caius Laelius, commonly called the Wise, when he was praetor, crippled and reduced, and so subdued his ferocity that he transmitted an easy conflict with him to his successors. Since, then, the force of justice is such that it strengthens and augments the resources even of robbers, how great shall we account its efficacy among laws and courts, and in a well ordered state?

12. I am inclined to think, indeed, that not only among the Medes, as Herodotus relates,[2] but also among our ancestors, men who had borne a high moral character were in early times appointed kings, in

---

1. These men were hardly robbers in the ordinary sense of the word; but they carried on for many years guerilla warfare, and, as is generally the case in such warfare, their forays were fully as much predatory as murderous. They were called robbers because they were barbarians. But Bardylis is termed by Diodorus king of the Illyrians, having Pyrrhus, king of Epeirus, for his son-in-law; and Viriathus seems to have been a patriotic chieftain, whose prime aim was to resist the Roman supremacy.

2. According to Herodotus, Deioces, ambitious of sovereignty, commenced as arbitrator in his own village, and on account of the reputation thus obtained for justice was chosen king. His administration is represented as having been, though impartial, annoyingly inquisitorial and relentlessly severe. But as his reign began more than seven centuries before the Christian era, he may be regarded as a semi-mythical personage, and a like doubt may be thrown on the origin of the Median sovereignty. The theory of the

order to the administration of justice; for when the poor commonalty were oppressed by those of greater wealth, they had recourse to some one man pre-eminent in virtue, who, while he defended the poorer classes from wrong, by establishing equitable jurisdiction kept the highest under the same legal obligations with the lowest. There was like reason for making laws as for choosing kings; for equality of right was always sought, nor without equality can right exist. If this could be obtained through the ministry of one just and good man, the people were contented under his rule. But when this ceased to be the case, laws were invented which should speak with all, at all times, in one and the same voice. This, then, is manifest, that those of whose justice the mass of the people had an exalted opinion used to be chosen as rulers. If in addition these same persons were thought wise, there was nothing that men did not expect to obtain under their administration. Justice is, therefore, by all means to be cherished and held fast, at once for its own sake—else it would not be justice—and for the increase of one's honor and fame.

But as there is a method, not only of acquiring money, but also of investing it, so that it may supply constant demands for generous giving no less than for necessary uses, so is fame to be properly invested as well as sought. There is great truth, however, in the saying of Socrates, that this is the nearest way, and, as it were, a short road to fame,—for one to endeavor to be such as he would wish to be regarded. If there be those who think to obtain enduring fame by dissembling and empty show, and by hypocrisy, not only of speech, but of countenance also, they are utterly mistaken. True fame strikes its roots downward, and sends out fresh shoots;[1] all figments fall speedily, like blossoms, nor can anything feigned be lasting. Very many cases might be cited in attestation on either side; but for the sake of brevity I will name but a single family. Tiberius Gracchus, the son of Publius, will be praised as long as the memory of Roman affairs shall last; but his sons were not approved by good men while they were living, and in death they have their position among those whose murder was justifiable.[2]

---

origin of kingly power here given seems to have been a favorite notion with Cicero, and is found in other works of his. It perhaps defines what ought to have been; but in fact the kingly office was probably at the outset but an extension of patriarchal sovereignty.

1. The allusion here seems to be to trees like the banyan, whose branches, as they bend to the ground, take root, and send up fresh shoots.

2. All the surviving records of the father's life entirely justify Cicero's encomium; it is

13. Let him, then, who would obtain genuine fame discharge the duties of justice. What these are I have shown in the First Book.

But in order that we may be taken for what we really are, though there is the greatest efficacy in our being what we would be taken for, yet some additional rules are to be given. If, indeed, one from early youth finds himself in a position of celebrity and reputation, either inherited from his father (as I think is the case with you, my Cicero,) or by some chance or happy combination of circumstances, the eyes of all are turned to him; inquiry is made about him, what he is doing, how he is living, and, as if he were moving in the clearest light, nothing that he says or does can be concealed. But those whose first years, on account of their lowly and obscure condition, are passed out of the knowledge of men, as soon as they emerge from childhood, ought to hold great aims in view, and to strive after them with unswerving diligence, which they will do with the greater confidence, since that age is not only exempt from envious regard, but is even looked upon with favor.

A youth, then, has the first title to fame, if he have the opportunity of obtaining it by military service, in which many in the days of our ancestors won early distinction; for wars were almost perpetual. But your time of service fell upon the epoch of that war in which one party was exceedingly guilty, the other unsuccessful. Yet in this war, when Pompey had made you commander of the left wing of his army,[1] you won great praise both from that illustrious man and from your fellow-soldiers for your horsemanship, your skill in the use of weapons, and your endurance of all the hardships of the camp and the field. This reputation of yours sank, indeed, simultaneously with the state. I have undertaken this discussion, however, not with reference to you alone,

---

an open question whether the sons may not have fully inherited his high moral worth and devoted patriotism. The family was plebeian, and it may not be otherwise than natural, that while the father—allied by marriage to the patrician family of the Scipios—was identified with the aristocracy, the sons should with honest and disinterested zeal have devoted themselves to the relief, elevation, and well-being of the plebeians, who in their time might justly complain of disabilities and oppression.

1. Latin, *alae alteri. Ala* may mean either one of the wings of an army or one of the squadrons of cavalry usually attached to every legion of foot-soldiers in service. Without the *alteri*, as young Cicero was only sixteen years of age, *alae* should undoubtedly be rendered *a squadron*, and many of the commentators suspect *alteri* to be a spurious interpolation. But as Pompey was to the last degree solicitous to secure and retain the moral support of Cicero, he may have sought to flatter the father by appointing the son to a nominal command, delegating its more important duties to officers of maturer years and experience.

but with reference to young men as a class. Let us then pass on to the remaining subjects.

As in all other respects mental are much greater than bodily achievements, so those things which we accomplish by intellect and reason win greater favor than those which we perform by mere physical strength. The first claim that can be proffered for the general esteem proceeds from regularity of conduct, with filial piety and kindness to those of one's own family. Then, too, young men become most favorably known when they seek the society of eminent, wise, and patriotic citizens, with whom if they are intimate, they inspire the people with the expectation that they are going to resemble those whom they have chosen as models for imitation. His frequenting the house of Publius Mucius[1] gave the youth of Publius Rutilius[2] the reputation both of moral purity and of legal knowledge. On the other hand, however, Lucius Crassus, while yet a mere boy, sought no countenance from his elders, yet won for himself the highest reputation from that splendid and famous accusation;[3] and (as we learn was the case with Demosthenes),[4] at the very age when young men are wont to be applauded for their exercises in declamation, Lucius Crassus showed that he could already do to perfection before the judges what it would have been to his credit to have merely rehearsed by way of practice at home.

14. But while there are two kinds of speech, to one of which conversation belongs, to the other public debate,[5] there is no doubt that the latter is most conducive to the acquisition of fame (for it is that which

---

1. Publius Mucius Scaevola, of the highest reputation as a jurist, and a copious writer on the Roman law. While vehemently opposed to the Gracchi, and approving of the murder of Tiberius Gracchus, he gave a legal opinion in favor of compensation from the public treasury for the value of the effects constituting the dowry of the wife of Caius Gracchus, lost in the popular disturbance caused by her husband.

2. A man of rigid integrity and probity, and eminent for ability and learning as a jurisconsult and a forensic orator.

3. Lucius Licinius Crassus. He was undoubtedly the greatest orator of his time. Cicero may have heard him, having been sixteen years of age at his death. When a mere stripling,—Tacitus says, of nineteen years,—he accused Caius Papirius Carbo, of what crime we do not know, probably of bribery or extortion, and met with such signal success that Carbo committed suicide to escape condemnation.

4. Demosthenes, at the age of eighteen, brought a successful suit against his guardians, to compel them to render account of his property in their hands.

5. Latin, *contentio*. The only occasions for the practice of oratory in Rome were such as might be designated by this term, which means *contention*. They were the advocacy of disputed measures in the Senate or before the people and the pleading of cases in the courts of law.

we dignify by the name of eloquence); yet it is hard to say to what a degree agreeableness and affability of conversation win favor. There are extant letters of Philip to Alexander, of Antipater to Cassander, and of Antigonus to Philip,—all three, as we learn, men of the greatest practical wisdom,—in which they advise their sons to allure the minds of the multitude in their favor by kindliness of address, and to charm the soldiers by accosting them in a genial way.

But the speech that is uttered with energy in a great assembly often awakens the enthusiasm of the entire audience; for great is the admiration bestowed on him who speaks fluently and wisely, and those who hear him think that he also has more intelligence and good sense than other men. And if there is in the speech substantial merit united with moderation, there can be nothing more worthy to be admired, especially if these properties are found in a young man. But while there are many kinds of occasions that demand eloquence, and many young men in our state have obtained praise by speaking both before judges and in the Senate, the highest admiration attends the eloquence of the courts,[1] before which there are two descriptions of oratory, that of accusation, and that of defence, of which, although the latter is more worthy of praise, yet the former is very frequently regarded with favor. I spoke just now of Crassus. Marcus Antonius[2] did the same when he was a young man. A public accusation also brought into favorable notice the eloquence of Publius Sulpicius,[3] when he arraigned for trial that seditious and worthless citizen, Caius Norbanus. Yet this ought not to be done often, nor ever except in the interest of the state, as in the cases that I have named, or to avenge wrongs, as the two Luculli did,[4] or for those under one's special patronage, as when I appeared

---

1. There was in Rome no profession corresponding to that of the modern advocate. There were jurisconsults, men learned in the law, many of whom were also eloquent advocates, while others were chamber-counsel, to whom advocates, as well as the immediate parties in a suit, resorted for legal opinions and advice. But any man who had the will and the ability might take charge of a case in court; and for young Romans who aspired to distinction, after military ambition began to wane, the bar was the favorite avenue to the popular favor. There were no public prosecutors; but any person who was ready to make and sustain a criminal charge had only to present himself before the *praetor urbanus*, and to swear that he was acting not from malicious motives, but in good faith, and in the interest of the state.

2. Grandfather of the triumvir,—a contemporary of Crassus, and of nearly equal reputation as an orator.

3. He was twenty-eight years old when he accused Caius Norbanus of *majestas*, or treason, for turbulent and seditious conduct as tribune of the people.

4. The augur Servilius had prosecuted their father for bribery and malversation

in behalf of the Sicilians,[1] and Julius[2] in behalf of the Sardinians in the accusation of Albucius the propraetor. The painstaking fidelity of Lucius Fufius in the accusation of Manius Aquillius[3] is also well known. One may, then, venture upon accusation once, or, at any rate, not often. Or if there be reason for doing so more frequently, let it be done as a service to the state, whose enemies one is not to be blamed for punishing repeatedly. But even then let there be a limit; for it is the part of a hard man, or, I should rather say, scarcely of a man, to prefer a capital charge against any considerable number of persons.[4] While it is fraught with personal danger, it is also damaging to one's reputation, to allow himself to be called an accuser, which was the fortune of Marcus Brutus,[5] born of an illustrious race, the son of the Brutus who was eminent for his skill in the civil law. Moreover, this maxim of duty is to be carefully observed, that you never bring an innocent person to a capital trial; for this cannot possibly be done without guilt. Nay, what is so inhuman as to pervert eloquence, bestowed by Nature for the security and preservation of men, to the destruction and ruin of good citizens? On the other hand, we are not to be so scrupulous as to decline defending on some occasions a guilty man, if he be not utterly depraved and false to all human relations. This the people demand, custom permits, even humanity endures. It belongs to the judge in the cases before him always to seek the truth; to the advocate, sometimes to defend the probable, even if it be not absolutely true,—which I should not dare to write, especially in a philosophical treatise, unless that strictest of the Stoics, Panaetius, were of the same opinion. But fame and favor are best secured by the defence of accused persons, especially if it so happens that this service is rendered in aid of one who seems

---

in Sicily, and procured his condemnation and exile. Though the elder Lucullus was undoubtedly guilty, his sons may have supposed him innocent, and at any rate they avenged themselves by the unsuccessful impeachment of Servilius.

1. In the impeachment of Verres.

2. Caius Julius Caesar, who commenced public life by the accusation of Titus Albucius of extortion as praetor in Sicily, and procured his condemnation.

3. He was accused by Fufius of extortion in Sicily; but, notwithstanding strong proofs of guilt, was acquitted on the ground of signal courage and ability in military command.

4. *Judicium capitis*, or a capital trial, was a phrase used, not only where life was put in jeopardy, but with reference to all cases in which one's standing and privileges as a citizen were imperilled, and the danger of degradation or exile was incurred.

5. Marcus Junius Brutus. His father was eminent for his legal learning. Of the son we know little except from Cicero, who may have been prejudiced against him as belonging to the opposite political party.

to be circumvented and put in peril by the influence of some man in power,—a service which I have performed on many other occasions, and especially—when I was still a young man—in defending Sextus Roscius[1] against the power of Lucius Sulla, then playing the tyrant,—a speech which, as you know, is published.

15. Having explained the ways in which, consistently with duty, young men may obtain fame, I must speak, in the next place, of beneficence and liberality, of which there are two sorts, kindness to those needing it being shown either by personal service or by money. The latter is more easy, especially for one who is rich; but the former is more noble, more magnificent, and more worthy of a strong and eminent man. For although in both modes there is the generous desire of bestowing benefit, yet in the one case the kindness is drawn from the purse, in the other from the giver's own ability and worth. The bounty which proceeds from one's property drains the very source of liberality. Thus generosity is made impossible by generosity, which you can extend to the fewer in time to come, the more numerous its beneficiaries have been in the time past. But those who will be beneficent and generous in personal service, that is, by influence and effort, the more persons they have already benefited, will have the more helpers in doing good. Then, too, by the habit of beneficent action, they will be better prepared, and, as it were, better trained, to merit the gratitude of the larger number. Philip, in a certain letter of his, very justly blames his son Alexander for seeking the good will of the Macedonians by distributing gifts among them. "What, the mischief!" says he, "ever induced you to entertain a hope like this, that those whom you had corrupted by money would be faithful to you? Are you doing this that the Macedonians may hope to have you not for their king, but for their lackey and caterer?" "Lackey and caterer" is well said, since such conduct is mean for a king; and still better was it that he termed lavish giving "corruption." For he

---

1. There is nothing in the entire record of Cicero's life more honorable to him than his conduct on this trial, in which he was for the first time engaged in a criminal cause. Sextus Roscius was accused of the murder of his father, on no valid or probable evidence, and undoubtedly with the view of securing permanent legality to the seizure of the father's property on the false pretence of unpaid debts. The principal in the fraud and the instigator of the criminal pursuit was Chrysogonus, a freed man of Sulla. With every possible obstacle thrown in his way, and with the whole influence of the dictator pressed into the opposite scale, Cicero procured, by the masterly management of the case, no less than by his eloquent defence, the acquittal of his client, but undoubtedly incurred imminent peril.

who receives such gifts grows worse, and more ready to expect the like in all time to come. He said this to his son; let us regard his advice as given to all. It is, then, beyond doubt that the kindness which consists in personal service and effort is more honorable, and extends farther, and can benefit a larger number. Yet gifts must be sometimes bestowed, nor is this form of kindness to be wholly repudiated; and aid should be often given to the deserving poor from one's own property, but thriftily and moderately. Many, indeed, have squandered their property in inconsiderate generosity. But what is more foolish than to disable yourself from continuing to do what you take pleasure in doing? Moreover, rapine follows extravagance in giving; for when men in consequence of their lavish generosity have begun to be in want, they are constrained to lay hands on the property of others. Thus, while they desire to be generous in order to win favor, they obtain not so much the attachment of those to whom they have been liberal as the hatred of those whom they have robbed. Therefore private property should neither be so shut up that kindness cannot open it, nor so thrown wide as to lie open to all. Let a limit be observed, and let this be determined by our means. We ought always to remember what has been so often repeated by our people as to have come into use as a proverb, that prodigal giving has no bottom.[1] For what bound can there be to such giving, when those who have been accustomed to receive, crave what they have been wont to get, and others also crave the same?

16. Of bountiful givers there are, in fine, two kinds, the one class prodigal, the other liberal,—the prodigal, those who, in public banquets, distributions of flesh, gladiatorial shows, and the preparation of games and wild-beast fights, pour out money on the kinds of things of which they will leave but a brief remembrance, or none at all; the liberal, those who by their wealth redeem persons captured by robbers, or take upon themselves the debts of their friends, or render them aid in marriage-portions for their daughters, or help them in acquiring or increasing property. I therefore wonder what came into the mind of Theophrastus in the book that he wrote about Riches,[2] in which he said many things admirably well, but that to which I now refer, absurdly. For he is prolix in praise of the magnificence and elaborateness of popular

---

1. The allusion here is, undoubtedly, to the cask with a perforated bottom which the Danaides are eternally attempting to fill.
2. A lost book.

entertainments, and regards the means of meeting such expenses as the chief advantage of wealth. But in my mind the advantage derived from the liberality of which I have given a few examples seems much greater and more certain. How much more soberly and justly does Aristo of Ceos[1] reprove us for not being surprised at these outpourings of money which are made to propitiate the multitude! "If those besieged by an enemy," he says, "are forced to pay a pound[2] for a pint[3] of water, at the first hearing it seems incredible and all are amazed; yet when they consider the case they excuse it on the plea of necessity; but in this immense waste and these boundless expenditures we feel no great astonishment, and that too, though neither is want thus relieved nor respectability enhanced, and the very delight of the multitude is transient and lasts but a little while, and, withal, is felt only by the most fickle, whose memory of the enjoyment expires as soon as they are satiated." He fittingly concludes that "these things are gratifying to boys, and weak women, and slaves, and to free men who bear the nearest resemblance to slaves; but that they cannot by any means be approved by a serious man and one who weighs what is done by fixed principles." Yet I am aware that in our city it is an old tradition, and one that has come down from good times, that lavishness in the aedileship may be expected even from the best men.[4] Thus Publius Crassus, rich equally in his surname and in his estate, gave the most costly public entertainments in his aedileship, and shortly afterward Lucius Crassus, with Quintus

---

1. Latin (in many of the best editions), *Aristo Ceus;* (in all extant manuscripts and early editions) *Aristoteles.* Aristotle not only has no sentiment like this in his extant writings, but can hardly have had in his time the material for such a description of senseless extravagance. The public entertainments of his age, especially in Athens, while redolent of superior culture, were comparatively inexpensive. Aristo of Ceos wrote a treatise (now lost) on Vain Glory (περὶ κενοδοξίας), from which this passage may very probably have been quoted. But the reading which gives his name is at best an ingenious and not unlikely conjecture.

2. *Mina*, in value a little more than four pounds sterling.

3. *Sextarius*, about a pint.

4. Of course, popularity in an aedileship contributed largely to one's success as a candidate for higher offices, and in the best days of the republic an aspirant for the popular favor may, as aedile, have made for the entertainment of the public an expenditure fully level with his ability. But before Cicero's time it had become common for an aedile to incur in that office heavy debts, to be liquidated, if ever, when as propraetor or proconsul he should be able to fill his exchequer with provincial spoils. Debts thus contracted were regarded as an obligatory mortgage on the popular suffrage, by which the debtor should have the opportunity of reimbursing himself for his outlay to please the people.

Mucius, the most moderate of all men, for his colleague, served through a most magnificent aedileship; and in like manner Caius Claudius, the son of Appius, and many afterward, the Luculli, Hortensius, Silanus. Publius Lentulus, when I was consul, surpassed all that went before him. Scaurus imitated him. But the entertainments given by my friend Pompey in his second consulship were the most magnificent. With reference to all these matters you see what my opinion is.

17. Yet the suspicion of penuriousness must be avoided. Mamercus, a very rich man, by declining to be a candidate for the aedileship, lost his election as consul. If such expenditure, then, is demanded by the people, and though not desired, at least approved by good citizens, it is to be incurred, yet in proportion to one's ability, as in my own case;[1] and if at any time some end of great importance and value can be gained by largesses to the people, they may be bestowed, as in the recent instance in which Orestes gained great honor by a public dinner in the streets under the name of a tithe-offering.[2] Nor did any one find fault with Marcus Seius, because in a time of dearth he gave the people corn for a penny[3] a peck;[4] for he thus freed himself from great and inveterate odium by a lavishness not unbecoming inasmuch as he was an aedile, and not very extravagant. But it was to the highest honor of my friend Milo when, not so very long ago, by gladiators bought for the sake of the state which was dependent on my safety, he suppressed all the plots and mad endeavors of Publius Clodius.[5] There is, therefore, sufficient reason for profuseness, if it is either necessary or useful. Yet in expenditures of this sort the rule of moderation is the best. Lucius Philippus, indeed, the son of Quintus, a man of great genius and of the highest eminence, used to boast that, without giving any public entertainment, he had been elected to all the offices that were regarded as the most honorable. Cotta said the same; so did Curio. I can

---

1. Cicero, as aedile, gave three public games.

2. The Romans frequently offered to some god, generally to Hercules, a tithe of their property on the eve of any great enterprise, or of their gains, in case of any signal success. But a small part of such an offering was consumed in sacrifice, and the rest was commonly utilized for a magnificent public festival. The words *polluceo* and *polluctura* as applied to such feasts may authorize the supposition (though I know of no other ground for it) that Pollux may have had in earlier time the honor which was subsequently paid to Hercules.

3. *As*, about half an English penny.

4. *Modius*, a little less than a peck.

5. Clodius was undoubtedly the greater ruffian and the worse man of the two; but it is only by shutting out all testimony save that of Cicero's magnificent defence of Milo, that we can regard him as a pre-eminently law-abiding and patriotic citizen.

also to a certain extent[1] make the same boast; for, as compared with
the importance of the offices which I obtained without any opposing
votes[2] in the years at which I became eligible[3] to them respectively,—
which was not the case with either of those whom I have named,—
the expense of my aedileship was very small. At the same time, the
more desirable expenditures in connection with public office are for
moles, docks, harbors, aqueducts, and whatever may be of service to the
community. Although what is given personally, as it were, into men's
hands, confers more immediate gratification, the expense incurred
in public works is more thankworthy. I blame the cost bestowed on
theatres, porticos, new temples, with diffidence on account of my regard
for Pompey's memory;[4] but the wisest authorities disapprove of such
expenditures, as did this very Panaetius whom in my present treatise
I have followed, not translated; as did also Demetrius Phalereus, who
finds fault with Pericles for throwing away so much money on that
famous vestibule of the Parthenon.[5] But this entire subject is carefully
discussed in my book on the Republic.[6] The whole system of such
extravagant largesses, in general worthy of censure, is under certain
circumstances necessary,—yet, when it becomes necessary, the expense
must be apportioned to one's means, and kept within moderate limits.

18. In the other style of free expenditure which proceeds from liberality, we ought not to be equally ready to give where the cases are
unlike. The case of him who is laboring under misfortune differs from
that of him who, without any actual stress of adverse circumstances,
seeks to improve his condition. Generosity ought to be more readily
bestowed on the unfortunate, unless perchance they deserve what they
suffer. Yet with regard to those who desire assistance, not to be saved
from utter ruin, but to reach a higher position, we ought to be by no

---

1. Cicero never attained the censorship, to which, by custom tantamount to constitutional law, and seldom departed from, ex-consuls alone were eligible.
2. The vote was taken by centuries, so that a large opposing minority might be
consistent with a nominally unanimous suffrage.
3. The normal age at which one was eligible to the quaestorship was thirty; to the
aedileship, thirty-seven; to the praetorship, forty; to the consulship, forty-three. These
rules had sometimes been disregarded, but were generally adhered to.
4. Pompey erected the most splendid of the then existing theatres, and temples to
Venus and Victoria.
5. The Propylaea, said to have cost a sum equivalent to two millions of our money.
6. This discussion is not found in any of the portions of the *De Re Publica* that have
been recovered.

means niggardly, but to be judicious and careful in selecting suitable subjects for our bounty. For Ennius says very fittingly:—

"Good done amiss I count as evil done."

But what is given to a good and grateful man yields us in return a revenue both from him and from others. For when one does not give at haphazard, generosity confers the highest pleasure, and most persons bestow upon it the greater applause, because the kindheartedness of any one who holds a conspicuous station is the common refuge for all. Care must be taken, therefore, that we confer on as many as possible benefits of such a nature that their memory may be transmitted to children and posterity, so that they too cannot be ungrateful. All, indeed, hate him who is unmindful of a benefit received, and think themselves wronged when generosity is thus discouraged; and he who is thus ungrateful becomes the common enemy of persons of slender fortunes.[1] Moreover, the liberality of which I now speak is of service also to the state in redeeming captives from slavery, and in providing needy persons with the comforts of life, which used to be very commonly done by men of senatorial rank,[2] as we find written out in full in the speech of Crassus.[3] This habitual practice of charity I regard as far preferable to the giving of public shows. The former is the part of substantial and prominent citizens; the latter seems to belong to those who fawn on the people, and tickle, so to speak, the fickleness of the multitude by low pleasure. But it will be becoming for one, while munificent in giving, to be also not severe in exacting, and in all contracts, in selling and buying, in hiring and leasing, in questions arising out of adjoining houses and estates,[4] to be fair and accommodating, freely

---

1. Injustice is done to Cicero when these interested motives to beneficence are regarded as standing alone. It must be remembered that in the First Book the duty of beneficence is urged on grounds of intrinsic right; while expediency is the express and sole subject of the Second Book, in which it is his aim to show that interest and duty point in the same direction,—that the selfish man sins against himself no less than against his neighbor.

2. So long as there was a wide distinction between the orders of the Roman state, the patricians, in general, took a generous care of the interests of their respective clients and dependents. Indeed, the very term *patrician* is an enduring record of kindly relations between the higher and the lower orders.

3. Lucius Licinius Crassus (§ 13). The reference is undoubtedly to his speech in favor of the restoration of judicial functions from the *equites* to the Senate.

4. There were subtleties in the Roman law as to the falling of water from the eaves of houses (*stillicidium*), the preservation or obstruction of light, and various matters of

making concessions from his own right, avoiding litigation as much as he can without excessive sacrifice, and perhaps even beyond what might seem the proper limit. For it is not only generous, but sometimes profitable also, to abate a little from one's rightful claims. Yet reference must be had to one's own estate, which cannot be suffered to go to ruin without disgrace to the owner; but private property must be so cared for as to leave no suspicion of penuriousness and avarice. Indeed, the ability of being generous without robbing one's self of his patrimony is the greatest revenue that money can yield. Theophrastus also rightly commends hospitality; for it is, as it seems to me, very becoming that the houses of distinguished men should be open to distinguished guests; and it is even for the honor of the state that foreigners should not lack this kind of liberality in our city. It is also in the highest degree expedient for those who desire to obtain great influence by honorable means to avail themselves of help and favor among foreign nations through their guests. Theophrastus, indeed, says that Cimon, at Athens, was hospitable not to strangers only, but to all of his own district of Laciadae,[1] making such arrangements and giving such orders to his farm-servants, that every attention should be shown to any citizen of that district who might turn aside to his country residence.

19. But the benefits which are bestowed, not by gift, but by personal service, are conferred, sometimes on the whole state, sometimes on individual citizens. To protect the rights of others, to aid them by legal advice, and by this sort of knowledge and skill to be of service to as many as possible, tends very largely to the increase of one's influence and popularity. Thus among many things to be commended in the days of our ancestors, it is worthy of note that the knowledge and the interpretation of our admirably constituted civil law were always held in the highest honor. This science, until the present unsettled times, the leading men of the state retained as one of their special prerogatives. Now, as is the case with civil offices and with all grades of rank, its prestige is destroyed, and this the more shamefully, as it took place

---

dispute that might arise and in all time do arise between owners of contiguous houses. Between estates outside of the city there was legally a space of five or six feet in which each owner had a right of way, and neither a right of occupancy for his own uses. Rights of way and other easements were attached, also, to many private estates. Hence a fruitful field for litigation.

1. The territory of Attica (including Athens) was divided into one hundred and seventy-four δῆμοι, or districts. The *demos* of Laciadae was outside of the city.

in the lifetime of him who would have transcended in legal learning
all his predecessors whom he equalled in rank.[1] This kind of service,
then, is gratifying to many, and is adapted to bind men by the ties of
benefit. Closely allied to skill in interpreting the law is oratory, which
even surpasses it both as a grave pursuit and as a personal accomplish-
ment. For what stands before eloquence, whether in the admiration
of its hearers, the hope of those who need its aid, or the gratitude of
those defended by it? To this, therefore, our ancestors assigned the
first rank among civil professions. There is, then, an extended range
of beneficial services and of patronage open to the eloquent man, who
willingly appears in the courts, and, as was the custom in the time of
our fathers, without reluctance and without compensation[2] defends
the causes of the many who seek his aid. The subject was reminding
me to deplore here, as elsewhere in my writings, the discontinuance,
not to say the extinction, of eloquence,—only I should dread the appearance of making complaint in my own behalf. But yet we see how
many orators have passed away, in how few is there good promise,
in how much fewer ability, in how many nothing save presumption.
Yet while not all, indeed only a few can be either skilled in the law
or eloquent, still one may render service to many, by canvassing in
their behalf for appointments, by appearing in their interest before
judges and magistrates, by watching the progress of their cases in court,
and soliciting for them the aid of legal counsellors and of advocates.
Those who do thus, obtain the largest amount of good will, and their
labor has a most widely extended influence. Nor need they here to be
admonished (for it is obvious), that they take heed lest while they desire
to assist some, they disoblige others. For under such circumstances they
are liable to hurt the feelings of those whom it is either morally wrong
or inexpedient for them to wound. If they do this unwittingly, it is
the result of carelessness; if knowingly, of recklessness. You must even
resort to apology wherever you can, to those to whom you unwillingly
give offence, showing them why what you did was necessary, so that you

---

1. Servius Sulpicius, after the death of Mucius Scaevola the most learned and celebrated jurisconsult. He died but a year before this treatise was written, and Cicero
pronounced a eulogy on him in the Senate.
2. The Roman law prohibited advocates from taking fee or reward. There is no proof
that Cicero was ever paid directly or indirectly for his services as an advocate, though
undoubtedly presents and legacies from those who had enjoyed the benefit of his services
may have been among the sources of his wealth.

could not have done otherwise, and promising them that the omission shall be compensated by other services and kind offices.

20. But while in giving assistance to men reference is usually had either to character or to condition, it is easy to say, and men commonly do say, that in conferring[1] favors they are influenced by the character, not by the outward condition of their beneficiaries. This mode of speaking sounds well. Yet who is there, who in rendering his service does not prefer the cause of a rich and influential man to that of a man without influence, though of signal excellence? Our will, for the most part, inclines the more strongly toward him from whom we may expect the more prompt and speedy remuneration. Yet we ought to look more carefully at the nature of things. Undoubtedly that poor man, if he is a good man, even if he cannot return the favor, can bear it faithfully in mind; and it is well said, whoever he be that first said it, "He who has money has not repaid it; he who has repaid it has it not: but he who has returned kindness has it, and he who has it has returned it." Now those who think themselves rich, respectable, fortunate, are unwilling to be placed under obligation by kindness rendered, nay, they even think that they have bestowed a favor when they have received one however great, and they imagine that something is also demanded or expected of them,—still more, it seems to them as bad as death to have it said that they are indebted to any one's patronage, or to be called any one's clients. On the other hand, the man of slender means just spoken of, thinking that whatever is done for him is done from regard to himself, not to his outward condition, endeavors to appear grateful, not only to him who has deserved his thanks, but also,—for he needs many helpers,—to those from whom he expects similar favors. Nor, if perchance he can render some good office in return, does he magnify it, but rather underrates it in what he says about it. This also is to be observed, that if you defend a rich and successful man, the favor does not extend further than to the man himself, or, peradventure, to his children; while if you defend a poor, yet upright and self-respecting man, all men of humble condition who are not bad—and there is a great proportion of these among the people—see in you a defence prepared for their exigencies. Therefore I think a kindness better invested with good men than with men of

---

1. Latin, *collocandis*, investing, i.e., conferring favors with a view to the revenue in influence and popularity which they may bring in return.

fortune. In fine, we should endeavor to meet the claims of those of every class; but if it come to a competition between rival claimants for our service, Themistocles may be well quoted as an authority, who, when asked whether he would marry his daughter to a good poor man, or to a rich man of less respectable character, replied, "I, indeed, prefer the man who lacks money to the money that lacks a man." But the moral sense is corrupted and depraved by the admiration of wealth. Yet of what concern to any one of us is another man's great fortune? Perhaps it is of benefit to him who has it,—not always, however. But suppose it to be of benefit to him,—he may, indeed, have more to spend; but how is he made any better? If, however, he be really a good man, let not his wealth be a hindrance, only let it not be a motive for your serving him. The decisive question must be, not how rich one is, but what sort of a man he is. But the ultimate rule in conferring favors and rendering service is, never to make any effort against the right, or in behalf of the wrong; for the basis of enduring praise and reputation is justice, without which there can be nothing worthy of commendation.

21. Having now spoken of the kinds of good offices that concern individuals, I must next discuss those which have reference to a body of men and to the state. Of these a part are such as accrue to the benefit of the whole community; a part, such as affect individuals, though in the form of public service. Both interests ought certainly to be cared for, that of individuals no less than of the community at large, yet in such a way that what is done may be of benefit, or at all events, not of injury to the state. The distribution of corn by Caius Gracchus[1] was excessive, and tended to drain the public treasury; that of Marcus Octavius[2] was moderate, and both within the easy ability of the state and necessary to the people,—therefore a beneficial measure both to the individual citizens who received the public bounty and to the state. He who administers the affairs of the state must take special care that every man be defended in the possession of what rightfully belongs

---

1. Caius Gracchus, as tribune of the people, procured the passage of a law by which every resident of the city who should personally appear at the Capitol might buy five *modii* (or pecks) of corn each month, at less than half the average price, therefore at much less than cost. The tendency, and of course a prime object, of this measure was to bring into the city, and under the influence of the popular leaders, large numbers of the poorer population in the rural districts.

2. Tribune of the people not long after Caius Gracchus. He procured the passage of a law raising the price of corn from the public granaries to a rate which arrested the depletion of the treasury.

to him, and that there be no encroachment on private property by public authority. Philippus, during his tribunate, when he proposed the agrarian law (which he readily suffered to be rejected, behaving in the matter with great moderation), while in defending the measure he said many things adapted to cajole the people, did mischief by the ill-meant statement that there were not in the city two thousand men that had any property. It was a criminal utterance, tending to an equal division of property, than which what more ruinous policy can there be? Indeed, states and municipalities were established chiefly to insure the undisturbed possession of private property; for though under the guidance of Nature men were brought together, still it was with the hope of guardianship for their property that they sought the defence of cities. Pains should also be taken that there may be no need of levying a tax on property,[1] which in the time of our ancestors was often done on account of the poverty of the treasury and the frequency of wars. Against such a contingency provision should be made long beforehand. But in case such a tax should be necessary for any state—for I would rather speak thus than forebode evil for our own state, and I am treating not of our own, but of states in general—pains must be taken to make all the citizens understand that in order to remain secure they must yield to this necessity. Moreover, it will be the duty of those who govern the state to take care that there be a full supply of everything requisite for the public service. How this provision is commonly made and how it ought to be made, there is no need of discussing,—it is a perfectly plain matter; the subject required to be merely alluded to.

But the chief thing in every department of public business and official administration is that even the least suspicion of greediness for money be put at rest. Caius Pontius,[2] the Samnite, said, "Oh that Fortune had reserved me and delayed my birth till the time, should it ever come, when the Romans had begun to take bribes! I would not then have suffered them to hold their supremacy any longer." Many generations must, indeed, have been waited for; for only of late this evil has invaded

---

1. For one hundred and four years, from the close of the Macedonian war (B. C. 147), which brought an immense amount of treasure into the public coffers, till the very year succeeding Cicero's death, no property-tax was levied, the spoils of war and the tribute from the provinces sufficing for the public expenditure.

2. The Samnite general who defeated the Roman army at the Caudine Pass, and many years later was himself defeated by Quintus Fabius Maximus, taken prisoner, led in triumph, and beheaded.

our state. Therefore I am glad that Pontius lived then rather than now, if indeed he was so much of a man. It is not yet a hundred and twenty years[1] since Lucius Piso's law about extortion was passed, whereas there had been no such law before. But there have since been so many laws each more severe than the preceding, so many accused, so many penally sentenced, so great an Italian war[2] caused by fear of judicial proceedings, such a pillaging and plundering of our allies[3] when laws and courts were suspended, that we owe what strength we have to the weakness of others, not to our own virtue.

22. Panaetius praises Africanus because he abstained from all illicit gain. Why should he not praise him? There were in him other greater qualities; the merit of abstaining from illicit gain belongs not only to the man, but to those times. Paulus obtained all the immense treasure of Macedonia. He brought so much money into the public treasury, that the booty acquired by that one commander put an end to the property-tax. But to his own house he brought nothing save the eternal memory of his name. Africanus imitated his father, being none the richer for the overthrow of Carthage. What think you? Was Lucius Mummius, his colleague in the censorship, any the richer when he had destroyed to its foundations a city of vast wealth?[4] He chose to embellish Italy rather than his own house;[5] though indeed in the embellishment of Italy his house also seems to me more truly embellished. There is, then,—to return to the point whence I made this digression,—no fouler vice than the greed of money, especially in the case of the leading citizens who

---

1. About a century and a half after the death of Pontius.

2. Commonly called the Social War. Marcus Livius Drusus had, while tribune of the people, procured the passage of a law providing for inquiry into the corrupt practices of the courts, which had in many instances acquitted persons justly charged with bribery and extortion. He had also procured the passage of laws conferring certain privileges— with a view to ultimate citizenship—on the Italian allies. The Senate, under the influence of those who feared an honest judiciary, annulled all the laws that had been enacted under the auspices of Drusus, on the pretext that they had been carried against the auspices, and in defiance of certain provisions by statute requiring a seventeen days' promulgation of laws before they could be passed, and forbidding the massing of several distinct clauses in the same vote. The allies were, of course, thwarted of their expectations, and hence the Social War.

3. During the dictatorships of Sulla and Caesar.

4. Corinth.

5. He flooded Rome with the richest spoils of Grecian art; but though by no means a man of pure life, he rigidly abstained from participating in the booty or gain of his conquest. Pliny says of him, that he filled the city with trophies of conquered Achaia, yet left not a dowry for his daughter.

govern the state; for to turn the state into a source of profit is not only vile, but even outrageous and execrable. Thus the oracle which the Pythian Apollo pronounced,

> "*By naught but greed of gain will Sparta perish,*"

he seems to have proclaimed not to the Lacedaemonians alone, but to all rich nations. But by no means can those who preside over public affairs more readily conciliate the favor of the multitude than by abstinence from the acquisition of wealth and the moderate use of what they have.

Those, therefore, who desire to be popular, and with that view either attempt agrarian measures,[1] that the occupants of the public domains may be driven from their homes, or advocate the remission of debts,[2] are undermining the foundations of the state,—in the first place, harmony, which cannot exist when money is taken from some and debts are cancelled for others; in the next place, equity, which is utterly destroyed, if hindrances are laid in the way of men's keeping their own property. For, as I said above, this belongs to the very idea of a state and a city, that the protection of every man's property should be certain and not a subject of solicitude. Moreover, by measures thus ruinous to the state men do not gain the favor that they anticipate. He from whom property is taken becomes their enemy. He to whom it

---

1. The agrarian laws that have so large a place in Roman history are often misunderstood in consequence of a misapprehension of the Latin terms *possessor* and *possessio*. These laws proposed the eviction, in many instances, of possessors, but not of owners. *Possessio* means not ownership, but occupancy. The lands obtained by conquest were for the most part leased on what were understood to be and what we should call perpetual leases, on condition of the payment of one tenth or one fifth of the annual revenue of the estate into the public treasury,—a condition which after a time lapsed into disuse and oblivion, so that the lands thus acquired were transmitted, bequeathed, and sold, as freeholds would have been, and with no expectation that the possession would ever be disturbed. The possessors thus had the consciousness of ownership, and the sympathy of the aristocracy and the rich men, on their side; and though the state, having never ceded the fee of its domain, had, no doubt, a right to take its lands from defaulting tenants and give them to the veterans or the landless plebeians, still this could not be done without the commission of virtual wrong to a large extent, and perhaps reducing to utter penury some who had felt as secure in the possession of their property as if it had come down to them in an unbroken line of inheritance from the beginning of time. We thus can reconcile the by no means delusive show of right and humanity on the face of the agrarian laws with the virtuous detestation expressed for them by not a few law-abiding Romans.

2. *Novae tabulae*, or the general remission or scaling down of debts, was, in the latter days of the Roman republic, a frequent demand of demagogues and of their followers and dupes.

is given conceals his desire to receive it, and especially in the case of debt cancelled, hides his joy, lest he may be suspected of having been insolvent. On the other hand, he who is wronged remembers it, and keeps his grievance in full sight.[1] Nor if those to whom property is wrongfully given are more numerous than those from whom it has been unjustly taken, are they therefore possessed of more influence; for these matters are determined, not by number, but by weight. But what justice is there in a proceeding by which he who had no landed estate obtains an estate that has been in the possession of the same family for many years, or even generations, while he who has had the estate loses it?

23. It was for wrongs of this sort that the Spartans banished Lysander the ephor, and put to death Agis the king,[2] the first instance of the kind; and from that time such dissensions ensued that tyrants sprang up, and men of high rank were expatriated, and that most admirably constituted state fell to pieces. Nor did it fall alone, but overthrew also the remainder of Greece by the contagion of evils which, starting from the Lacedaemonians, spread from state to state. What more? Did not agrarian agitations destroy our citizens the Gracchi, sons of that most eminent man Tiberius Gracchus, grandsons of Africanus? On the other hand, praise is most justly bestowed on Aratus of Sicyon, who, when his state had been kept under oppression by tyrants for fifty years,[3] going

---

1. These words of Cicero describe with wonderful accuracy the result of an experiment with *novae tabulae* in the United States of America. A profligacy at which Rome in her worst days might have blushed found expression in a national bankrupt law passed by Congress in 1841, repealed in 1843. By this law fraudulent insolvency had every possible facility and inducement. There were in every community notorious instances in which men who had paid little or nothing except the required legal fees showed openly and shamelessly the property of which they had cheated their creditors. In fine, any man who chose to do so, whatever his pecuniary ability, could repudiate his debts. The law resulted in the collapse and defeat of the very party that had hoped by means of it to consolidate its power. Those who had taken the benefit of the law were ashamed of it when they needed it no longer; while those whom it had wronged had no tolerance for the authors of their wrong,—thus verifying to the letter what Cicero says about the effect of such measures on the popularity of their authors and abettors.

2. Agis, the fourth Spartan king of the name, under whose government the Lysander here referred to was ephor. Their endeavor was to procure the entire cancelling of debts, and the re-distribution of the Spartan territory.

3. With only a brief interval, during which the father of Aratus had served as one of two chief magistrates chosen by the people. He probably was not in power long enough, or had not sufficient authority, to right the wrongs committed by a series of tyrants. He was killed by a usurper when Aratus was seven years old, and in the interval of thirteen years before the successful expedition of Aratus, that usurper and his successor had been slain, so that Nicocles was the third in this latter series of tyrants.

from Argos to Sicyon, obtained possession of the city by entering it secretly, and after suddenly crushing the tyrant Nicocles, restored six hundred exiles who had been the richest men in the state, and freed the people by his advent. Then when he came to reflect on the difficulty about property and its occupancy, thinking it very unjust that those whom he had restored and whose estates were in the possession of others should remain poor, and at the same time deeming it hardly fair that possessions of fifty years' standing should be disturbed, because after so long a time many estates were innocently held by inheritance, many by purchase, many by dowry, he determined that neither ought the property to be taken from those in possession, nor ought the former owners to be left without compensation. Having come to the conclusion that there was need of money to set this matter right, he said that he wanted to go to Alexandria, and ordered everything to remain as it was till his return. So he hastened to Ptolemy, who had been his host, the second king after the building of Alexandria. Having explained to him his purpose to restore freedom to his country, and informed him of the posture of affairs, this man most worthy of celebrity easily obtained from the rich king the aid of a large amount of money. Carrying this to Sicyon, he took into his counsel fifteen of the principal men, with whom he considered carefully the cases both of those who held the property of others, and of those who had lost their own property, and managed by a valuation of the estates to persuade some of the present occupants to resign their estates and accept money instead, and others to account it more to their advantage to have the value of their estates paid to them than to recover possession of them. Thus it was brought about that all went their ways perfectly satisfied, without any ground of mutual complaint. O truly great man, well worthy to have been a native of our own commonwealth! Thus it is fitting to deal with citizens; not, as we have twice seen, to plant the spear in the market-place, and to submit the property of citizens to sale by the auctioneer. That Greek, indeed, as was to have been expected of a wise and excellent man, thought that the welfare of all should be consulted; and this is the consummate reason and wisdom of a good citizen, not to create separate interests among those of the same state, but to hold all together by the same principles of equity. May men live without compensation on the estates of others? Why so? That when I have bought, built, keep the estate in good order, spend money upon it, you without my consent may have the use of what is mine? What else is this but to take from some what is their own, and to give to others what is not their own? Then too, what does the cancelling of debts mean, but that you may buy an estate with my money, and keep it, while I go without the money?

24. Therefore the care should be to check such excessive indebtedness as will be of injury to the state (which may be prevented in many ways),[1] and not, if there are debts, to deprive the rich of their money, and to let the debtors gain what is not theirs. For nothing holds the state more firmly together than good faith, which cannot possibly exist unless the payment of debts is obligatory. Never was there a more earnest endeavor against the payment of debts than in my consulship. The attempt was made by arms and military operations, and by men of every kind and order, which I resisted with such energy that so dire a calamity was averted from the state. Never was there a larger amount of debt, nor was it ever discharged more fully or more easily; for when the hope of successful fraud was removed, the necessity of paying was the consequence. He indeed, of late conqueror, but at that time conquered,[2] carried out what he had then planned after he had ceased to have any personal interest in it.[3] So great was his appetite for evil-doing, that the very doing of evil gave him delight, even when there was no special reason for it. From this kind of generosity, then,— the giving to some what is taken from others,—those who mean to be guardians of the state will refrain, and will especially bestow their efforts, that through the equity of the laws and of their administration every man may have his own property made secure, and that neither the poorer may be defrauded on account of their lowly condition, nor any odium may stand in the way of the rich in holding or recovering what belongs to them; while they will also aid the growth of the state in power, territory, and revenue, by whatever means, military or domestic, may be at their command. Such are the aims of truly great men; these

---

1. Cicero would undoubtedly have said, by sumptuary laws, which were sanctioned by the imperfect political economy of that day.

2. Cicero undoubtedly suspected, and with good reason, that Caesar had covertly abetted the Catilinian plot, and Caesar's speech in the Senate, if its tone and spirit are fairly represented in Sallust's report of it, shows that he was solicitous to save the lives of the conspirators.

3. At the time of Catiline's conspiracy Caesar was very deeply in debt. He, in the first year of his dictatorship, was the author of a law by which debts were liquidated by payment of seventy-five per cent of their amount, the pretext being the increased value of money occasioned by the expenditure and loss of treasure during the civil war. Caesar himself had by that time become, not only free from debt, but absolutely rich, in great part, no doubt, from the perquisites of his Gallic campaigns.

things were wont to be done in the times of our ancestors; and those who perform faithfully duties of this class will with the greatest benefit to the state secure for themselves distinguished favor and reputation.

Among these precepts relating to expediency, Antipater of Tyre, a Stoic, who recently died at Athens, thinks that two subjects were omitted by Panaetius,—the care of health and that of money,—which, I suppose, were passed over by that illustrious philosopher, because they presented no difficulty. They certainly belong under the head of expediency. I would say, then, that good health is maintained by the knowledge of one's own constitution, by observing what things are wont to be salutary or injurious, by self-restraint in the whole manner and habit of living, by abstaining from sensual indulgences, and, lastly, by the skill of those to whose profession these matters belong. Property ought to be obtained in ways not dishonorable, to be preserved by diligence and frugality, to be increased also by the same means. These things Xenophon, the disciple of Socrates, has thoroughly discussed in his book on Domestic Economy,[1] which, when I was about of your present age, I translated into Latin.

25. But the comparison of things that are expedient—this being the fourth division, omitted by Panaetius—is often necessary. For bodily endowments are wont to be compared with outward advantages, and outward advantages with bodily endowments, bodily endowments themselves, too, with one another, and outward advantages, some with others. Thus in comparing bodily endowments with outward advantages, you would rather be in good health than rich; in comparing outward advantages with bodily endowments, you would choose to be rich rather than to possess extraordinary strength of body. In comparing bodily endowments among themselves, good health would be preferred to sensual gratification, strength to swiftness of foot; and of outward advantages, fame to wealth, city revenues[2] to country revenues.[3] Of this last kind of comparisons is that quoted from the elder

---

1. *Oeconomicus* (Οἰκονομικός), a work wholly devoted to the administration of the household and private property.

2. From rents, and from the wages of slaves,—this last a very lucrative and therefore a favorite source of income, though not deemed entirely respectable.

3. Returns at a lower percentage than city investments, and more precarious, as contingent on the character of the season and the abundance or scantiness of the crops. Agriculture, though not the most gainful, was regarded as the most respectable source of income.

Cato, who, when asked what was the most profitable thing to be done
on an estate, replied, "To feed cattle well." "What second best?" "To
feed cattle moderately well." "What third best?" "To feed cattle, though
but poorly." "What fourth best?" "To plough the land." And when he
who had made these inquiries asked, "What is to be said of making
profit by usury?" Cato replied, "What is to be said of making profit by
murder?"[1] From this and from many things beside it may be inferred
that comparisons of things expedient are not infrequently made, and
that this is rightly added as a fourth head to our discussion of duty.
But in everything appertaining to this last topic, the acquisition and
investment of money,—I could wish, as to its use, too,—the discussions
that might be held by certain very good men sitting among the bankers
in the Exchange[2] are worth more than those by any philosophers of any
school. Yet these matters ought to be taken notice of; for they belong
under the head of expediency,—the subject of this book. Let us, in the
next place, pass on to what remains of the proposed plan.

---

1. Usury was held in abhorrence even more than in contempt.
2. Latin, *ad Janum medium*. Janus was the name of a street in or near the forum, in
which were to be found almost all the brokers' and bankers' offices in the city; and *Janus
summus, medius,* and *imus* meant, respectively, the top, middle, and bottom of Janus
Street.

Book III

1. My son Marcus, Cato, who was nearly of the same age[1] with Publius Scipio, the first of the family that bore the name of Africanus, represents him as in the habit of saying that he was never less at leisure than when he was at leisure, or less alone than when he was alone,—a truly magnificent utterance and worthy of a great and wise man, indicating that in leisure he was wont to think of business[2] and in solitude to commune with himself,[3] so that he was never idle, and had no need betweenwhile[4] of another person's conversation. Thus the two things, leisure and solitude, which with others occasion languor, quickened his energies. I could wish that I were able to say the same; but if I cannot by imitation attain such transcendent excellence of temperament, I at any rate in my inclination make as near an approach to it as I can; for, debarred from political and forensic employments by sacrilegious arms and violence, I am abandoning myself to leisure, and therefore, leaving the city and wandering from one place in the country to another, I am often alone. But neither is this leisure of mine to be compared with the leisure of Africanus, nor this solitude with his. He, indeed, reposing from the most honorable public trusts, upon certain occasions snatched leisure for himself, and from the company and concourse of men betweenwhile betook himself to solitude as to a harbor. But my leisure proceeds from lack of employment, not from desire for repose. For, the Senate being silenced[5] and the courts suspended,[6] what is

---

1. About ten years younger.
2. Latin, *otio* de *negotiis* = *nec-otiis*.
3. Latin, in *solitudine* secum loqui *solitum*.
4. Latin, *interdum*, literally, betweenwhile.
5. Antony had surrounded the Senate in its sessions with armed followers of his, and of course the purpose, as well as the effect of so doing, was to repress freedom of utterance.
6. Brutus and Cassius, both praetors, could not safely remain in or return to the city, and as they were legally at the head of the judiciary, the courts were suspended.

there worthy of myself that I can do either in the senate-house or in the forum? Thus, after having lived in the greatest publicity and in the presence of my fellow-citizens, I now hide myself to escape the sight of bad men who swarm everywhere, and I am often alone. Yet since philosophers say that one ought not only of evils to choose the least, but from even these least evils to extract whatever of good there may be in them, I therefore am utilizing my leisure, though it be not that to which I was entitled after having obtained leisure[1] for the state, nor am I suffering this solitude—which necessity, not choice, imposes upon me—to remain idle. Africanus, indeed, as I think, attained a higher merit; for no monuments of his genius were committed to writing, there remains no work of his leisure, no fruit of his solitude,—whence it should be inferred that it was in consequence of mental activity and the investigation of those things to which he directed his thoughts, that he was never at leisure or alone. But I who have not such strength of mind that I can abstract myself from the weariness of solitude by silent meditation, am directing all my study and care to this labor of writing, and thus in the short time that has elapsed since the overthrow of the state, I have written more than in many years while it stood.[2]

2. But while all philosophy, my Cicero, is fertile and fruitful, nor is any part of it untilled or unoccupied, there is no department within its pale more productive or more prolific than that relating to the duties whence are derived rules for living consistently and virtuously. Therefore, although I trust that you are diligently hearing and receiving instruction on this subject from Cratippus, the foremost philosopher of the present age, yet I think that it will be for your benefit that your ears should constantly ring with such themes, and, were it possible, should hear nothing else. While this should be the case with all who mean to enter on a virtuous life, I am inclined to think that there is no one for whom it is more fitting than for you,—liable as you are to no small anticipation of imitating my diligence, to the confident expectation that you will succeed me in public trusts, and to some hope, perhaps, of rivalling my reputation. You have, beside, taken upon yourself the heavy responsibility of both Athens and Cratippus, to which and to

---

1. Latin, *otium. Repose* would be a better rendering, were it not that we should lose Cicero's play upon *otium*, which is broad enough in its meaning to apply to the repose of the state from the plots of conspirators no less than to the rest of a worker from his labor.

2. Almost all Cicero's philosophical and rhetorical works were written in the last three or four years of his life.

whom, after resorting as to a mart of good culture, it would be in the last degree shameful for you to return empty-minded, thus disgracing the reputation of both the city and the master. Look to it, then, that you accomplish as much as you can aim after in purpose, and strive for by labor,—if learning be labor rather than pleasure,—nor suffer it so to be, that when I have given you the most liberal supplies,[1] you may appear to have been false to your own interest. But enough of this; for I have written to you much and often by way of exhortation. Let us now return to the remaining head of my proposed division.

Panaetius, then, who without doubt discussed the subject of duty with the utmost precision, and whom I have thus far followed for the most part, with an occasional correction, having laid down three heads under which men were wont to reason and deliberate concerning duty,—one, the inquiry whether the act under discussion is right or wrong, the second, whether it is expedient or inexpedient, the third, the mode of settling the discrepancy in case what has the appearance of right is repugnant to what seems expedient,—treated of the first two heads in three books, and said that he would speak of the third head in its turn, but failed to keep his promise. I am the more surprised at this, because Posidonius, his pupil, says that he lived thirty years after writing those first three books. I am surprised, too, to find this head but slightly touched upon in certain essays of Posidonius, especially as he says that there is no subject of so essential importance in all philosophy. I by no means agree with those who maintain that this subject was not overlooked by Panaetius, but purposely omitted, and that it ought not to have been written upon at all, inasmuch as expediency can never be in conflict with the right. With regard to this assertion one thing admits of doubt, whether this third head of Panaetius ought to have been taken into consideration or entirely omitted; the other thing admits of no doubt, that it was undertaken by Panaetius, but left unwritten; for to him who has finished two heads of a threefold division the third of necessity remains. Besides, at the close of his third book he promises to treat of this division in its turn. We have further the testimony of Posidonius, a credible witness, who also writes in one of his letters that Publius Rutilius Rufus, a pupil of Panaetius, used to say that as no painter could be found who would finish the part of the Venus of

---

1. Young Cicero's annual allowance would amount in our money to a little more than four thousand dollars.

Cos[1] which Apelles had left imperfect—the beauty of the countenance
putting it beyond hope that the rest of the body could be finished so as
to bear comparison with it—so no one had attempted what Panaetius
had left incomplete, on account of the surpassing excellence of the
things that he had completed.

3. There can, then, be no doubt about the intention of Panaetius; but
whether he was right or not in annexing this third head to his discussion
of duty may, perhaps, admit of doubt. For whether the right is the sole
good, as the Stoics think, or whether, as your Peripatetics maintain, the
right is the supreme good in such a sense that all things else placed in
the opposite scale are of insignificant moment, it is beyond question
that expediency can never clash with the right. Thus we learn that
Socrates used to denounce as worthy of execration those who regarded
as separable the expedient and the right, which are conjoined by nature.
The Stoics have agreed with him in maintaining that whatever is right
must be expedient, and that nothing can be expedient which is not right.
Now if Panaetius were the sort of man to say that virtue ought to be
cultivated because it is productive of utility, as those do who measure
the desirableness of objects by the pleasure or the freedom from pain
that they may afford, he might in that case have said that expediency is
sometimes repugnant to the right. But since he belongs to the class of
men who regard what is right as alone good, and consider life as made
neither better by the acquisition nor worse by the loss of those things
which with a certain show of expediency are in conflict with the right,
it does not seem as if he ought to have introduced a discussion in which
what appears to be expedient should be compared with what is right.
For what the Stoics term the supreme good, to live in conformity with
nature, means, as I think, to be always in harmony with virtue, yet to
make free choice among things in general that are in accordance with
nature, only on condition of their not being repugnant to virtue. Such
being the case, some think that this comparison is not properly brought
forward, and that no practical lessons ought to have been given under
this head. Indeed, that which is properly and with literal truth called

---

1. The most admired of all the pictures of Apelles. He completed one picture of
Venus *Anadyomene* (or rising out of the sea) for the temple of Aesculapius at Cos, which
was afterward placed by Augustus in the temple which he built to Julius Caesar. This was
injured, and no one dared to repair it. The painter commenced another picture of Venus,
for the Coans, intending to surpass the previous one, but died before it was completed,
and it remained unfinished. It is probably to this that Cicero refers.

the right is found in the wise alone, nor can it ever be separated from virtue; while in those not possessed of perfect wisdom, the perfect right itself cannot possibly be, but only semblances of the right. For all these duties discussed in the present treatise—contingent,[1] as the Stoics call them—are common, and are largely practised, and many attain to them by excellence of natural disposition and by advancement in knowledge. But that duty which the Stoics term the right is perfect and absolute, and, in the phrase of those same philosophers, has all the numbers,[2] nor can it come into the possession of any one except the wise man. But when anything is done in which contingent duties are manifest, it seems to be abundantly perfect, because people in general do not understand what in it is wanting to perfection, while so far as they do understand, they think nothing omitted. The like is of ordinary occurrence in poems, pictures, and many other matters, namely, that the unskilled view with delight and commendation things that do not deserve praise, because, I suppose, there is in them something good of a kind to take the fancy of the ignorant, who are incapable of determining what defect there may be in the several objects thus placed before them; while after they have been taught by experts, they readily change their opinion.

4. These duties which I am discussing in the present treatise the Stoics call a sort of second-grade duties, not belonging to the wise alone, but common to them with the whole human race. Thus all in whom there is a virtuous disposition are favorably inclined to them. Nor, indeed, when the two Decii or the two Scipios are commemorated as brave men, or when Fabricius is called just, is the example of fortitude sought from them, or of justice from him, as from men in the strict sense of the term "wise;" for neither of them was wise as we would have the word "wise" understood. Nor yet were the men who were esteemed and surnamed Wise, Marcus Cato and Caius Laelius, wise in this sense, nor

---

1. Latin, *media*, which, literally translated, conveys no meaning. *Contingent* expresses, perhaps, as well as any single word the Stoic conception of the ordinary duties performed by persons not philosophers. The truly wise or ideal man (for the extreme Stoics denied that he had ever existed) discerned the absolute right in its very essence, by direct intuition. Other men performed duties, not because they were intrinsically right, but because each specific act of duty had for them its rule or law in external circumstances.

2. Most commentators say that the allusion here is to the rhythmical movements in dancing and gymnastic exercises, in which he who was perfect was said to have or to keep all the numbers. It seems to me more probable that Cicero refers to the Pythagorean doctrine of numbers, specific numbers denoting perfection of specific kinds, and "all the numbers" designating absolute perfection.

yet those famous seven;[1] but from their constant practice of common duties they bore to a certain degree the semblance and aspect of wise men.[2] Therefore, while it is an error to compare the right properly so called with expediency when repugnant to it, at the same time that which is commonly called right, and is held sacred by those who want to be regarded as good men, should never be compared with external goods; and it is as incumbent on us to defend and preserve that right which is on a level with our apprehension, as it is on the wise to cherish the right properly and truly so called. Otherwise, if any progress toward virtue has been made, it cannot be maintained. Enough has now been said about those who are reputed as good men on account of the discharge of common duties. But those who measure everything by the standard of gain and personal convenience, nor are willing that these goods should be outweighed by virtue, are accustomed, in their plans of life, to compare the right with what they deem expedient; good men are not so accustomed. I therefore think that when Panaetius said that men are wont to hesitate in this comparison, he meant precisely what he said; for he said only that they were wont, not that they ought, to hesitate. And, indeed, it is in the utmost degree base not only to prize what seems expedient above what is right, but even to compare them with each other and to incline to doubt with regard to them. What is it, then, that is wont sometimes to occasion doubt and may seem worthy of consideration? I believe that if doubt ever occurs, it is as to the actual character of that which is under consideration; for it often happens, under special circumstances, that what is wont for the most part to be accounted as wrong is found not to be wrong. Let a case which admits of a wider application be taken by way of example. What greater crime can there be than to kill not only a man, but an intimate friend? Has one, then, involved himself in guilt by killing a tyrant, however intimate with him?[3] This is not the opinion of the Roman people, who of all deeds worthy of renown regard this as the

---

1. The seven sages of Greece,—Bias, Chilo, Cleobulus, Pittacus, Periander, Solon, and Thales.

2. There is a striking analogy between the ideal man of the Stoics whom man never saw, and the Christian ideal of humanity but once realized in human form, and with reference to which as incarnate the best Christians hold the same position that was held by the warriors, patriots, and sages here named with reference to the Stoic ideal.

3. The reference here is, obviously, to the friendly relation in which Brutus stood to Caesar.

most noble. Has expediency, then, got the advantage over the right? Nay, but expediency has followed in the direction of the right.

Therefore, that we may be able to discriminate without mistake, if at any time what we call expedient shall seem repugnant to what we conceive of as right, there must be established some general rule,[1] which if we recognize in the comparison of things, we shall never be false to our duty. But this rule shall be in close accordance with the method and system of the Stoics, whom I am following in this treatise, because though by the early Academics and by the Peripatetics who were formerly identical with them those things that are right are preferred to those that seem expedient, yet these themes are discussed in a loftier tone by those to whom both whatever is right is also expedient, and there is nothing expedient that is not right, than by those to whom anything right can be otherwise than expedient, or anything expedient otherwise than right. Moreover, my sect of the Academy gives me broad liberty, so that I have a right to defend whatever seems to me probable. But I return to the general rule.

5. For a man to take anything wrongfully from another, and to increase his own means of comfort by his fellow-man's discomfort, is more contrary to nature than death, than poverty, than pain, than anything else that can happen to one's body or his external condition.[2] In the first place, it destroys human intercourse and society; for if we are so disposed that every one for his own gain is ready to rob or outrage another, that fellowship of the human race which is in the closest accordance with nature must of necessity be broken in sunder. As if each member of the body were so affected as to suppose itself capable of getting strength by appropriating the strength of the adjacent member, the whole body must needs be enfeebled and destroyed, so if each of us seizes for himself the goods of others, and takes what he can from every one for his own emolument, the society and intercourse of men must necessarily be subverted. It is, indeed, permitted, with no repugnancy of nature, that each person may prefer to acquire for himself, rather than for another, whatever belongs to the means of living; this, however, nature does not suffer,—that we should increase our means, resources,

---

1. Latin, *formula.*

2. This is the general rule, or *formula,* referred to in § 4. It embraces all forms of wrong-doing from man to man, and thus extends to all offences under the second and third of Cicero's divisions of duty, but would not include sins under the first and fourth.

wealth, by the spoils of others. Nor is this so merely by the law of nature
and of nations; but also by those statutes of particular communities
on which the body politic in each state depends for its safety, it is in
like manner enacted that no one can be permitted to injure another
for his own benefit. It is to this that the laws look, it is this that they
mean, that the union of citizens shall be secure; and those who dissever
it they restrain by death, exile, imprisonment, fine. Moreover, much
more is this end effected by the reason inherent in nature, which is
the law of gods and of men, which he who wills to obey—and all will
obey it who desire to live according to nature—will never so act as to
seek what belongs to another and to appropriate to himself what he has
taken from another. For loftiness and largeness of soul, and therewith
affability, justice, kindness, are more in accordance with nature than
pleasure, than life, than wealth, to despise which and to count them as
naught when compared with the common good is the token of a great
and lofty mind. To take aught from another for one's own benefit is,
then, more opposed to nature than death, or pain, or any other adverse
experience. At the same time, it is more in accordance with nature
to assume the greatest labors and discomforts for the preservation
and succor of all nations, were it possible, imitating that Hercules
whom human gratitude, commemorative of his services, exalted to a
seat among the gods, than to live in isolation, not only free from all
causes of disturbance, but even in the fulness of sensual gratification,
abounding in resources of every kind, nay, even surpassing all others
in beauty and in strength. Therefore every man endowed with a mind
of superior excellence and brilliancy prefers the former to the latter
mode of life, whence it may be inferred that man, when obedient to
nature, cannot injure man. Still further, he who maltreats another that
he himself may obtain some benefit, either is unaware that he is acting
contrary to nature, or else thinks that poverty, pain, loss of children,
of kindred, of friends, is to be avoided rather than wrong-doing to a
fellow-man. If he is unaware that he is acting contrary to nature in
maltreating men, how are you to reason with one who takes away from
man all that makes him man? But if he thinks that wrong-doing ought
indeed to be shunned, but that death, poverty, or pain is much more to
be shunned, he errs in imagining any evil affecting the bodily condition
or property to be of greater consequence than moral evil.

6. This, then, above all, ought to be regarded by every one as an
established principle, that the interest of each individual and that

of the entire body of citizens are identical, which interest if any one appropriate to himself alone, he does it to the sundering of all human intercourse. And further, if nature prescribes this, that man shall desire the promotion of man's good for the very reason that he is man, it follows in accordance with that same nature that there are interests common to all. The antecedent is true; therefore the consequent is true. For this is absurd indeed which some say, that they would take nothing from a parent or a brother for their own benefit, but that it is quite another thing with persons outside of one's own family. These men disclaim all mutual right and partnership with their fellow-citizens for the common benefit,—a state of feeling which dismembers the fellowship of the community. Those, too, who say that account is to be taken of citizens, but not of foreigners, destroy the common sodality of the human race, which abrogated, beneficence, liberality, kindness, justice, are removed from their very foundations. And those who remove them are to be regarded as impious toward the immortal gods; for they overturn the fellowship established among men by the gods, the closest bond of which fellowship is the opinion that it is more contrary to nature for man to take anything from man for his own benefit than to endure all forms of discomfort, whether external, or bodily, or even mental, which leave room for the exercise of justice. For this one virtue is mistress and queen of all the virtues. One may perhaps say, "Should not then a wise man who is perishing with hunger take away food from another man who is good for nothing?" No, indeed, by no means; for my life is not of greater service to me than is such a disposition of mind as would preclude my injuring any one for my own benefit. What if a good man, to save himself from perishing with the cold, should rob of his clothes the cruel and savage tyrant Phalaris? May he do it? These matters are very easy of determination. If, indeed, you were to take anything from a perfectly worthless man merely for your own benefit, you would perform an inhuman act and one contrary to nature. If, however, you are a person capable, by prolonging your life, of rendering great service to the state and to human society, and for that reason you take something from another person, you would not be blameworthy. But except in such a case, each man must bear his own privations rather than take what belongs to another. Sickness, or poverty, or anything of this kind is not, indeed, more opposed to nature than is the appropriation or coveting of what belongs to another. But at the same time the dereliction of the common good is opposed to nature, for it is unjust; and therefore the very law of nature, which preserves and maintains the good of man, undoubtedly prescribes that the necessaries of life should be transferred from an inefficient and useless man to a wise, good, brave man, whose death would make a large deduction from the common good,—provided he effect the transfer in such a way that his self-esteem and self-love may not furnish a pretext for wrong-doing. In this way he will perform his duty with reference to the good of mankind and to the human fellowship of which I have so often spoken. Now as regards Phalaris the decision is very easy; for we[1] have no fellowship with tyrants, but rather the broadest dissiliency from them, and this whole pestiferous and impious class of men ought to be exterminated from human society. Indeed, as limbs are amputated when they are bloodless and virtually lifeless, and injure the rest of the body, so this beastly savageness and cruelty in human form ought to be cut off from what may be called the common body of humanity. Of this sort are all the questions in which duty is to be determined from circumstances.

7. Panaetius would, I think, have followed up topics of this kind, had not some accident or some other occupation frustrated his intention. Toward these very inquiries there may be drawn from his first three books many maxims, from which it can be clearly seen what is to be avoided on account of its immorality, and what is not to be avoided because not absolutely immoral.

But since I am, as it were, putting the topstone on a work incomplete, yet almost finished, as mathematicians are wont, instead of demonstrating everything, to ask that some things be admitted[2] in order to explain more easily what they want to prove, so I ask of you, my Cicero, to admit, if you can, that nothing except what is right is to be sought for its own sake. If, however, you cannot grant this without hindrance from the teachings of Cratippus, you can certainly admit that what is right is to be sought chiefly for its own sake. Either proposition is sufficient for my purpose; and now this, now that, seems the more probable, while no other proposition relating to this subject is in any degree probable. At the same time, Panaetius ought in the first place to be defended on this point; inasmuch as he said, not that expediency could ever be in conflict with the right,—for this he could not consistently

---

1. We, i.e., the Roman people. Cicero evidently has the death of Caesar in his mind.
2. Axioms, which in their very nature do not admit of proof.

say,—but that things that seemed expedient might be thus in conflict. Indeed, he often affirms that nothing is expedient which is not also right, and nothing right which is not also expedient; and he maintains that no more prolific source of evil has ever found its way into human society than the opinion of those who have divorced the expedient and the right. Therefore, it was not in order that on certain occasions we should prefer expediency to the right, but that we might discriminate without mistake between appearance and reality, if at any time there were a seeming conflict, that he introduced into the plan of his work a seeming, not an actual, collision between the expedient and the right. This division, then, which he left unwritten, I propose to fill out, relying on no authority, from my own resources;[1] for since the time of Panaetius there has been nothing written on this head of a nature to satisfy me, among the works that have come into my hands.

8. When any specious appearance of expediency is presented, one cannot help being impressed by it. But if, when you give it closer attention, you see that there is something morally wrong connected with what thus seems expedient, in that case you are not to sacrifice expediency, but you are to understand that where there is moral wrong expediency cannot be. For if nothing is so contrary to nature as immorality (inasmuch as nature craves things right, and fitting, and consistent), and nothing so in unison with nature as expediency, then it is certain that expediency and immorality cannot exist in the same thing.[2] Still further, if we were born for virtue, and the right either is alone worthy to be sought (as Zeno maintained), or is assuredly to be regarded as immeasurably outweighing all things else (as is Aristotle's doctrine), then, of necessity, what is right must be either the sole or the supreme good. But what is good is certainly expedient. Consequently whatever is right is expedient.[3] It is then the misapprehension of bad men which, when it

---

1. Latin, *sed, ut dicitur, Marte nostro*, literally, "But, as the saying is, by my own Mars," i.e., fighting my own battle, depending on myself alone.
2. This was undoubtedly intended as a syllogism,—a favorite mode of statement or argument among the Stoics. It would admit of several logical forms, among others, of the following:—
Expediency is in harmony with nature;
Immorality is not in harmony with nature;
Therefore, what is immoral is not expedient.
—A syllogism in Camestres.
3. Another syllogism, in Barbara:—
Whatever is good is expedient;

lays hold on anything that seems expedient, considers it independently of the question of right. This is the origin of assassinations, poisonings, forgeries of wills. Hence come thefts, embezzlements of public money, plunderings and pillagings of allies and of citizens. Hence, too, proceed the intolerable usurpations of excessive wealth, and, lastly, even in free states, the yearning for sovereign authority, than which nothing can be imagined more foul or more offensive. Men, indeed, in their false appreciation, see the profit of the wrong they do; they see not the punishment, I do not say, of the laws which they often evade, but of the guilt itself, of which the punishment is intensely bitter. Therefore let no quarter be given to this class of doubters, utterly wicked and impious, who deliberate whether they shall pursue what they see to be right, or shall knowingly defile themselves with guilt; for there is crime in the mere hesitation, even if they do not go so far as the outward act. Therefore those things in which the very deliberation is criminal ought not to be deliberated at all. Moreover, the hope and expectation of concealment, whether of the act or of the actor, ought to be excluded from every deliberation on the conduct to be pursued. If we have made even the least proficiency in philosophy, we ought to be thoroughly persuaded that, even though we could escape the view of all gods and men, still nothing ought to be done by us avariciously, nothing unjustly, nothing lustfully, nothing extravagantly.

9. For this reason Plato introduces the wellknown story of Gyges,[1] who, when the ground had caved away on account of heavy rains, passed down into the opening, and saw, as the story goes, a brazen horse with doors in his sides. Opening these doors, he saw a man of unusual size, with a gold ring on his finger, which drawing off, he put it on his own finger (he was a shepherd in the king's service), and then repaired to the company of the shepherds. There, as often as he turned the part of the ring where the stone was set to the palm of his hand, he became invisible, yet himself saw everything; and was again visible when he restored the ring to its proper place. Then, availing himself of the advantage which the ring gave him, he committed adultery with the

---

Whatever is right is good (either the sole or the supreme good);

Therefore, whatever is right is expedient.

1. Herodotus makes Gyges, not a shepherd, but the prime minister of Candaules, King of Lydia, and writes that he killed Candaules and succeeded to the kingdom by the queen's connivance and aid. The story of the ring Plato quotes as a tradition, and makes the same use of it in the Second Book of the Republic that Cicero makes of it here.

queen, and by her assistance killed the king his master, and removed by death those whom he thought in his way. Nor could any one see him in connection with these crimes. By means of the ring he in a short time became king of Lydia. Now if a wise man had this ring, he would not think himself any more at liberty to do wrong than if he had it not; for it is right things, not hidden things, that are sought by good men. Here, however, certain philosophers, by no means ill-disposed, yet somewhat deficient in acuteness, say that this is only a fictitious and imaginary story that Plato has told,—as though, forsooth, he asserted that such a thing took place or could have taken place. The meaning of this ring and of this example is as follows: If no one would ever know, if no one would ever suspect, when you performed some act for the sake of wealth, power, ascendency, lust,—if it would remain forever unknown to gods and men, would you do it? They say that it is impossible. Yet it is not utterly impossible. But I ask, If that were possible which they say is impossible, what would they do? They persist, awkwardly indeed; they maintain that such a thing could not be, and they stand firm in this assertion; they do not take in the meaning of the phrase, "If it were possible." For when we ask what they would do if they could conceal what they did, we do not ask whether they can hide it; but we put them, as it were, on the rack, that if they answer that they would do what seemed expedient if assured of impunity, they may confess themselves atrociously guilty; and if they make the contrary answer, that they may grant that whatever is wrong in itself ought to be shunned. Let us now return to the subject under discussion.

10. There occur many cases of a nature to perplex the mind under the aspect of expediency,—cases in which the real question is not whether the right is to be sacrificed on account of the greatness of the benefit to be gained (for that is unquestionably wrong), but whether that which seems expedient can be done without guilt. When Brutus deposed his colleague Collatinus from the consulship, he might seem to have done this unjustly; for Collatinus had been the associate of Brutus, and his assistant in measures for the expulsion of the royal family. But when the chief men of the state had come to the determination that the kindred of Superbus, and the name of the Tarquins, and the remembrance of kingly government must be put out of the way, what was expedient— that is, care for the well-being of the country—was so entirely right that it ought to have satisfied Collatinus himself. Thus expediency became valid on account of the right that was in it, without which, indeed, there

could not have been any expediency. Not so, however, in the case of
the king who founded the city; for a bare show of expediency struck
his mind. When it seemed to him better to reign alone than with a
colleague, he killed his brother. He set aside both brotherly affection
and humanity, in order to attain what seemed expedient, yet was not
so; and then offered in defence the pretext of the wall,—a mere show
of right, improbable in itself, and insufficient even if true. He was
therefore entirely in the wrong. With his leave I would say it, whether
he be Quirinus or Romulus.[1] Nevertheless, advantages that are properly
our own we are not to abandon, or to yield up to others, if we ourselves
need them; but each one must minister to his own advantage only so
far as it may be done without wrong to others. Chrysippus,[2] who has
written many sensible things, wisely says: "He who is running a race
ought to endeavor and strive to the utmost of his ability to come off
victor; but it is utterly wrong for him to trip up his competitor, or to
push him aside. So in life it is not unfair for one to seek for himself what
may accrue to his benefit; but it is not right to take it from another."

But in the case of friendships there is the greatest perplexity as
to duty, it being equally opposed to duty to withhold what you can
rightfully concede to a friend, and to concede what is not right. Office,
wealth, pleasure, other things of that sort, are certainly never to be
preferred to friendship. At the same time a good man will do nothing
against the state, or in violation of his oath or of good faith, for the sake
of his friend, not even if he were a judge in his friend's case. For

"He drops the friend, when he puts on the judge."[3]

He will yield so far to friendship as to wish his friend's case to be
worthy of succeeding, and to accommodate him as to the time of trial
within legal limits. But inasmuch as he must pass sentence upon his
oath, he will bear it in mind that he has God for a witness, that is, as
I think, his own conscience, than which God himself has given man
nothing more divine. In this view, it is an admirable custom derived
from our ancestors—if we would only adhere to it—that when a favor
is asked of a judge, it is in the words, "So far as it can be done without

---

1. Whether he be god or man. Romulus was deified and worshipped under the name
of Quirinus.
2. A Stoic, and the most logical interpreter of the doctrines of the Stoic school.
3. A verse from an unknown poet.

a breach of good faith." A request proffered in such terms applies to things which, as I just said, can be granted by a friend who is acting as a judge. On the other hand, were one to feel bound to do all that friends might desire, such connections ought to be considered as not friendships, but conspiracies. I am speaking of ordinary friendships; for in the case of wise and perfect men there can be nothing of the kind. It is related that Damon and Phintias,[1] Pythagoreans, were so disposed toward each other, that when Dionysius the tyrant had fixed for one of them the day of execution, and he that was condemned to death asked for a few days' respite to make arrangements for the care of his family, the other became surety for his appearance, to die in his stead if he did not return. When he returned on the day appointed, the tyrant, admiring their mutual good faith, begged them to admit him to their friendship as a third person. In fine, whenever what seems expedient in friendship comes into competition with what is right, let the apparent expediency be disregarded; let the right prevail. Moreover, when in friendship things that are not right are demanded, religion and good faith are to take precedence of friendship. Thus will the choice of duty, which is the subject of our inquiry, be determined.

11. But it is in affairs of state that wrong is the most frequently committed under the show of expediency. Our own people were thus guilty with reference to the demolition of Corinth. The Athenians acted with still greater severity in decreeing that the men of Aegina,[2] who were able seamen, should have their thumbs cut off. This seemed expedient; for Aegina was too threatening on account of its proximity to the Piraeus. But nothing that is cruel is expedient; for cruelty is in the utmost degree hostile to human nature, which ought to be our guide. Those also are to be blamed who prohibit foreigners from living in their cities, and expel them, as Fannius did in the time of our fathers, and Papius more recently.[3] It is indeed right that one who is not a citizen should lack the full privileges of citizenship, as is enacted by the law passed under the consulship of those very wise men Crassus and Scaevola; but

---

1. Valerius Maximus writes this name Pythias.

2. This, if authentic, must have taken place in the fifth century before the Christian era. It is mentioned in no extant work of any Greek historian. It is related by Aelian, who, indeed, wrote in Greek, but was an Italian, lived as late as the reign of Hadrian, and embodied in his work floating traditions with authentic history.

3. Both of these men, in their respective tribunates, procured the passage of laws by which foreigners, temporarily resident in Rome, were compelled to leave the city.

it is clearly inhumane to prohibit foreigners from living in the city. On the other hand, a worthy renown rests upon the instances in which the show of public benefit is despised in comparison with the right. Our history is full of examples of this kind, while often at other times, especially in the second Punic war, when, after the disaster of Cannae, the people manifested greater spirit than ever in prosperity. There was no symptom of fear, no intimation of peace. Such is the power of the right, that it eclipses the show of expediency. When the Athenians were utterly unable to sustain the assault of the Persians, and determined that, deserting the city and leaving their wives and children at Troezen, they would go on board of their ships and defend the liberty of Greece by their fleet, they stoned to death a certain Cyrsilus who pressed upon them the advice to stay in the city and receive Xerxes. He, indeed, seemed to advocate expediency; but expediency did not exist, when the right was on the other side. Themistocles, after the victory in the Persian war, said in a popular assembly that he had a plan conducive to the public good, but that it was not desirable that it should be generally known. He asked that the people should name some one with whom he might confer. Aristides was named. Themistocles said to him that the fleet of the Lacedaemonians, which was drawn ashore at Gytheum, could be burned clandestinely, and if that were done, the power of the Lacedaemonians would be inevitably broken. Aristides, having heard this, returned to the assembly amidst the anxious expectation of all, and said that the measure proposed by Themistocles was very advantageous, but utterly devoid of right. Thereupon the Athenians concluded that what was not right was not expedient, and they repudiated the entire plan which they had not heard, on the authority of Aristides. Better this than our conduct in holding pirates free from all exactions,[1] our allies tributary.[2]

12. Let it be settled, then, that what is wrong is never expedient, not even when you obtain by it what you think to be of advantage to you. Nay, the mere thinking that what is wrong is expedient is in itself a misfortune. But, as I have already said, there often occur cases of such a nature that expediency seems in conflict with the right, so

---

1. After Pompey had suppressed piracy, the Cilician pirates whom he had subdued were formed into a flourishing colony, and subsequently entered into friendly and helpful relations with Antony.

2. The people of Marseilles, king Deiotarus, and, in fine, all the allies that had adhered to the Pompeian faction, were burdened with heavy tribute under Caesar's government.

that it must be ascertained by close examination whether it is really thus in conflict, or whether it can be brought into harmony with the right. Of this class are questions like the following: If, for example, a good man has brought from Alexandria to Rhodes a large cargo of corn, when there is a great scarcity and dearth at Rhodes and corn is at the highest price,—in case this man knows that a considerable number of merchants have set sail from Alexandria, and on his passage he has seen ships laden with corn bound for Rhodes, shall he give this information to the Rhodians, or shall he keep silence and sell his cargo for the most that it will bring? We are imagining the case of a wise and good man. We want to know about the thought and feeling of such a man as would not leave the Rhodians uninformed if he thinks it wrong, but who doubts whether it is wrong or not. In cases of this kind Diogenes of Babylon,[1] an eminent Stoic of high authority, is wont to express one opinion, Antipater[2] his pupil, a man of superior acuteness, another. According to Antipater, all things ought to be laid open, so that the buyer may be left in ignorance of nothing at all that the seller knows. According to Diogenes, the seller is bound to disclose defects in his goods so far as the law of the land requires, to transact the rest of the business without fraud, and then, since he is the seller, to sell for as much as he can get. "I have brought my cargo; I have offered it for sale; I am selling my corn for no more than others ask, perhaps even for less than they would ask, since my arrival has increased the supply. Whom do I wrong?" On the other side comes the reasoning of Antipater: "What say you? While you ought to consult the welfare of mankind and to render service to human society, and by the very condition of your being have such innate natural principles which you are bound to obey and follow, that the common good should be your good, and reciprocally yours the common good, will you conceal from men what comfort and plenty are nigh at hand for them?" Diogenes, perhaps, will reply as follows: "It is one thing to conceal, another not to tell. Nor am I now concealing anything from you, by not telling you what is

---

1. Diogenes was one of the three philosophers sent on an embassy from Athens to Rome (B. c. 155), to deprecate the payment of a heavy fine imposed on the Athenians. Aulus Gellius characterizes his eloquence as moderate and sober (*modesta et sobria*).

2. Little is known of Antipater, and of his works nothing remains; but from the incidental notices of his character and opinions, and of the reverence in which he and his memory were held, we have reason to believe that his opinions both in ethics and in theology were in advance of his age. He was the teacher of Panaetius.

the nature of the gods, or what is the supreme good,—things which it would profit you much more to know than to know the cheapness of wheat. But am I under the necessity of telling you all that it would do you good to hear?" "Yes, indeed, you are under that necessity, if you bear it in mind that nature establishes a community of interest among men." "I do bear this in mind. But is this community of interest such that one can have nothing of his own? If it be so, everything ought, indeed, to be given, not sold."

13. You see that in this whole discussion it is not said, "Although this be wrong, yet, because it is expedient I will do it;" but that it is expedient without being morally wrong, and, on the other side, that because it is wrong it ought not to be done. A good man sells a house on account of some defects, of which he himself is aware and others ignorant. Perhaps it is unhealthy, and is supposed to be healthy,—it is not generally known that snakes make their appearance in all the bedrooms,—it is built of bad materials, and is in a ruinous condition; but nobody knows this except the owner. I ask, if the seller should have failed to tell these things to the buyer, and should thus have sold his house for a higher price than he could have reasonably expected, whether he would have acted unjustly or unfairly? "Yes, he would," says Antipater; "for what is meant by not putting into the right way one who has lost his way (which at Athens exposed a man to public execration), if it does not include the case in which a buyer is permitted to rush blindly on, and through his mistake to fall into a heavy loss by fraudulent means? It is even worse than not showing the right way; it is knowingly leading another into the wrong way." Diogenes, on the other hand, says: "Did he who did not even advise you to buy, force you to buy? He advertised for sale what he did not like; you bought what you did like. Certainly, if those who advertise a good and well-built house are not regarded as swindlers, even though it is neither good nor properly built, much less should those be so regarded who have said nothing in praise of their house. For in a case in which the buyer can exercise his own judgment, what fraud can there be on the part of the seller? And if all that is said is not to be guaranteed, do you think that what is not said ought to be guaranteed? What could be more foolish than for the seller to tell the defects of the article that he is selling? Nay, what so absurd as for an auctioneer, by the owner's direction, to proclaim, 'I am selling an unhealthy house'?" Thus, then, in certain doubtful cases the right is defended on the one side; on the other,

expediency is urged on the ground that it is not only right to do what seems expedient, but even wrong not to do it. This is the discrepancy which seems often to exist between the expedient and the right. But I must state my decision in these cases; for I introduced them, not to raise the inquiry concerning them, but to give their solution. It seems to me, then, that neither that Rhodian corn-merchant nor this seller of the house ought to have practised concealment with the buyers. In truth, reticence with regard to any matter whatever does not constitute concealment; but concealment consists in willingly hiding from others for your own advantage something that you know. Who does not see what sort of an act such concealment is, and what sort of a man he must be who practises it? Certainly this is not the conduct of an open, frank, honest, good man, but rather of a wily, dark, crafty, deceitful, ill-meaning, cunning man, an old rogue, a swindler. Is it not inexpedient to become liable to these so numerous and to many more bad names?[1]

14. But if those who keep silence deserve censure, what is to be thought of those who employ absolute falsehood? Caius Canius, a Roman knight, a man not without wit and of respectable literary culture, having gone to Syracuse, for rest, as he used to say, not for business, wanted to buy a small estate, to which he could invite his friends, and where he could take his own pleasure without intruders. When his wish had become generally known, a certain Pythius, who was doing a banker's business at Syracuse, told him that he had a country-seat, not, indeed, for sale, but which Canius was at liberty to use as his own if he wished to do so; and at the same time he invited the man to supper at the country-seat for the next day. He having accepted the invitation, Pythius, who, as being a banker, was popular among all classes, called the fishermen together, asked them to fish the next day in front of his villa, and told them what he wanted them to do. Canius came to supper at the right time; a magnificent entertainment was prepared by Pythius; a multitude of little boats were in full sight; every fisherman brought what he had taken; the fish were laid down at the feet of Pythius. Then Canius says, "Prithee, what does this mean? So many fish here? So many boats?" And he answered, "What wonder? All the fish for the Syracuse market are here; they come here to be in fresh water. The fishermen cannot dispense with this villa." Canius, inflamed with longing, begs Pythius to sell the place. He hesitates at first. To cut the story short,

---

1. Latin, *vitiorum nomina*, literally, names of vices.

Canius over-persuades him. The greedy and rich man buys the villa for as high a price as Pythius chooses to ask, and buys the furniture too. He gives security; he finishes the business. Canius the next day invites his friends. He comes early; he sees not a thole-pin. He asks his next neighbor whether it is a fishermen's holiday, as he sees none of them. "Not so far as I know," was the reply. "No fishermen are in the habit of fishing here. I therefore yesterday could not think what had occurred to bring them." Canius was enraged. But what was he to do? My colleague and friend, Aquillius,[1] had not then published his forms of legal procedure in the case of criminal fraud, as to which when he was asked for a definition of criminal fraud, he replied, "When one thing is pretended, another done." This is perfectly clear, as might be expected from a man skilled in defining. Pythius, then, and all who do one thing while they pretend another, are treacherous, wicked, villainous. Therefore nothing that they do can be expedient, when defiled by so many vices.

15. But if the definition of Aquillius is correct, pretence and concealment should be entirely done away with. Thus a good man will neither pretend nor conceal anything for the sake of buying or selling on better terms. Indeed, this offence of criminal fraud had been previously punished both by the laws, as in the case of guardianship, by the Twelve Tables, and in the defrauding of minors, by the Plaetorian law,[2] and also, without express statute, by legal decisions in which the phrase "As good faith requires" is employed.[3] In other decisions the following words hold a prominent place:—in the case of arbitration about a wife's property, "The better, the more equitable;"[4] in the case of trust-property, "Fair dealing between good men."[5] What then? Can

---

1. Caius Aquillius Gallus was Cicero's colleague in the praetorship, and as the head of the judiciary introduced into his official edict, and thus into the body of the Roman law, important improvements in the legal remedies against criminal fraud (*dolus malus*).

2. This law (B. c. 192) first discriminated between minors (*minores*) under twenty-five years and those of age (*majores*). By this law fraud on minors was punished by a heavy fine and public infamy. It provided also that contracts with minors should be voidable, unless made with the consent of a guardian appointed by the praetor.

3. The text is slightly ambiguous, at least to a modern translator. Some commentators render the sentence as referring to decisions as to contracts in which the words *ex fide bona* are used; others, as referring to decisions in which these words are employed.

4. *Melius aequius*, prescribing, as I understand, a leaning in the wife's favor in any questions about the dowry to be restored in case of the wife's death, or, in that age more frequently, in case of her divorce.

5. *Inter bonos bene agier*, in the case of property conveyed to a trustee on condition of its being restored,—a condition sometimes to be inferred from the circumstances under which the conveyance was made rather than from the express terms of the contract.

there be any admixture of deceit in "The better, the more equitable?" Or when "Fair dealing between good men" is specified, can anything be done craftily or fraudulently? But, as Aquillius says, criminal fraud consists in misrepresentation. All falsehood, then, must be removed from contracts. The seller must not employ a sham purchaser, nor the buyer one to depreciate the article on sale by too low a bid. Let either party, if it comes to naming the price, say once for all what he will give or take. Quintus Scaevola, the son of Publius, when he asked to have the price of an estate that he was buying named once for all, and the seller had complied with his request, said that he thought it worth more, and added a hundred thousand sesterces.[1] There is no one who would say that this was not the act of a good man; but men in general would not regard it as the act of a wise man, any more than if he had sold an estate for less than it would bring. This, then, is the mischievous doctrine,—regarding some men as good, others as wise, according to which notion Ennius writes that the wise man who cannot provide for his own advantage is wise in vain. I would readily account this saying true, if I were agreed with Ennius as to what one's advantage is. I see, indeed, that Hecato of Rhodes, a disciple of Panaetius, says, in the books on Duties which he dedicated to Quintus Tubero: "It is a wise man's duty, while he does nothing contrary to morals, laws, and customs, to have regard to his private fortune. For we desire to be rich, not for ourselves alone, but for children, kindred, friends, and most of all for the state,—considering that the means and resources of individual citizens are the wealth of the state." The act of Scaevola just named cannot, then, be in any way pleasing to Hecato. Nor is any great praise or favor to be rendered to a man who merely says that he will not do for his own benefit what is unlawful. But if pretence and concealment constitute criminal fraud, there are very few transactions entirely free from criminal fraud; or if he is a good man who does good to those to whom he can and injures no one, of a certainty we shall not easily find that good man. We conclude, then, that it is never expedient to do wrong, because wrong-doing is always disgraceful; and because to be a good man is always right, it is always expedient.

16. As to landed property, the law of the state enacts that defects known to the seller must be made known in selling it; and while by

---

1. *Sestertii*, or one hundred *sestertia*, equivalent to between four and five thousand dollars of our money.

the law of the Twelve Tables it was enough for such things as were guaranteed to be made good, and for the seller who made false statements with regard to them to pay double damages, the jurisconsults have determined that the legal penalty applies also to reticence.[1] Their doctrine is, that whatever defect there may be in an estate, if the seller knows it, he is bound to make it good. Thus when the augurs were going to take an augury on the Capitol,[2] and had ordered Tiberius Claudius Centumalus, who had a house on the Coelian hill, to pull down those parts of it which were so high as to obstruct their view of the heavens, Claudius advertised the detached house, and sold it. The purchaser was Publius Calpurnius Lanarius. The same notice was given to him by the augurs. So when Calpurnius had complied with the order, and had ascertained that Claudius advertised the house for sale after being notified of the decree of the augurs, he procured the appearance of Claudius before a legally appointed arbitrator, suing him for damages for his breach of good faith. Marcus Cato pronounced the decision, the father of my friend Cato—for as other men are named from their fathers, so is the father of that illustrious man to be named from his son—he, I say, as judge, pronounced the decision: "Forasmuch as the seller knew of that decree when he sold the house, and did not make it known, the damage ought to be made good to the buyer." He thus decided that in good faith a defect known by the seller ought to be known by the buyer. If this was a right decision, then neither that corn-merchant, nor the seller of the unhealthy house, had a right to keep silence. But all such cases of reticence cannot be comprised in the law of the land, though those which can be so comprised are carefully repressed. Marcus Marius Gratidianus, my kinsman, had sold to Caius Sergius Orata the house which he had bought from that same Orata a few years before. The estate was subject to certain rights of way, which Marius had omitted to name in the contract of sale. The case was brought into court. Crassus was advocate for Orata, Antonius for Gratidianus. Crassus laid stress on the law that any defect known by the seller and not mentioned ought to be made good. Antonius rested his plea on the equity of the case, that inasmuch as the defect was not

---

1. This statement refers not to praetorian edicts or to judicial decisions, but to the interpretation of the statute by men learned in the law.

2. The augurs faced the east in taking their observations, so that a high house on the Coelian hill might obstruct their view, all the more so, if one of the augurs had any private grudge against the owner of the house.

unknown to Sergius, who had previously sold the house, there was no need of its being specified, nor had the purchaser been imposed upon, since he knew perfectly well to what the estate purchased was liable. To what purpose do I name these things? That you may understand that our ancestors did not approve of chicanery.[1]

17. But the laws remove chicanery in one way, philosophers in another,—the laws, so far as they can lay hold on overt acts; philosophers, so far as they can reach such cases by reason and understanding. Reason, then, demands that nothing be done ensnaringly, nothing under false pretence, nothing deceitfully. Yet is it not ensnaring to spread nets, even if you do not start and hunt your victims? For beasts themselves often fall into nets without being pursued. Is it not thus that you advertise a house,—put up a notice of sale as a net; sell the house on account of its defects; and some unwary person runs into the net? Yet such is the degenerate state of feeling, that I find this neither accounted as morally wrong, nor yet forbidden by statute or by the civil law, though it is forbidden by the law of nature. For there is—though I have often said it, there is need of its being said still oftener—a fellowship of men with men, which has, indeed, the broadest possible extent; a more intimate union, of those who belong to the same race; one closer still, of those who belong to the same state. Therefore our ancestors recognized a distinction between the law of nations and the law of the state. What is the law of the state is not necessarily also the law of nations; but whatever is the law of nations ought also to be the law of the state. But of true law and genuine justice we have no real and lifelike representation; their shadow and semblances alone are ours. Yet would that we might follow even these! For they are drawn from excellent models presented by nature and truth. How precious are these words: "That I be not taken in and defrauded through you or on account of my confidence in you!" What a golden formula is this: "As ought to be done between good men, fairly and without fraud!"[2] But the great question is, Who are the "good men," and what is it to be "fairly done"? Quintus Scaevola, the head of the pontifical college, said that there was the greatest force in all decisions to which the phrase "in good faith" was annexed, and he thought that as the term "good faith" had the broadest

---

1. Cicero here means to say: "Cases of this kind are comparatively recent. The records of the earlier and better times contain no such instances of chicanery."
2. These were forms used in deeds of trust.

application as employed in guardianships, partnerships, trusts, com-
missions, purchases, sales, hiring, leases, which make up the whole
system of social transactions, it required a judge of superior capacity to
determine—especially as there are often cross-suits—what each party
is bound to render, and to whom, in the satisfaction of just claims.

There should, then, be an end of chicanery and of that cunning which
means indeed to pass for prudence, but is an entirely different thing
and at the widest distance from it; for prudence has its proper place
in the choice between good and evil, while cunning—if whatever is
immoral is evil—prefers evil things to good.

Nor is it only with reference to landed estate that the civil law, derived
from nature, punishes cunning and fraud; but in the sale of slaves
also all fraud on the part of the seller is prohibited. By the edict of
the aediles,[1] the seller who may rightly be supposed to know about
the health, the truant habits, the dishonesty of the slave, is bound to
guarantee the purchaser against damage. The case of persons who sell
slaves that have recently come to them by inheritance is different.[2] From
these instances it is clear, since nature is the fountain of law, that
it is in accordance with nature that no one should act so as to prey
upon another's ignorance. Nor can there be found any greater source
of mischief to human society than the false show of intelligence in
the practice of cunning. Hence spring those countless cases in which
expediency seems to be in conflict with the right. For how few will
be found who, if impunity and absolute secrecy were offered, could
refrain from wrong-doing!

18. Let us, if you please, try the principle that I have laid down,
with reference to cases in which the generality of mankind do not
think that any wrong is committed. For I am not going to speak here
of assassins, poisoners, forgers of wills, thieves, peculators, who are
to be repressed, not by words and philosophical discussion, but by
chains and imprisonment. Let us consider the things that are done by
those who are accounted as good men. Certain persons brought from
Greece to Rome a forged will of Lucius Minucius Basilus, a rich man.
That they might more easily maintain its validity, they made joint-heirs
with themselves Marcus Crassus and Quintus Hortensius, the most

---

1. The regulation of the markets was among the functions of the aediles.
2. One who had just come into an inheritance of human chattels could not be expected
to know their characters and habits.

influential men of that time, who, while they suspected the forgery, yet being conscious of no guilt of their own in the case, did not spurn the paltry present that came to them through the crime of others. What then? Is their freedom from the positive offence of forgery sufficient for their acquittal? I think not, though I loved one of them while he lived,[1] and am not an enemy of the other now that he is dead.[2] But when Basilus meant that his sister's son, Marcus Satrius, should take his name, and had made him his heir,—I mean this patron of the Picene and Sabine territory, to the disgrace of our time,[3]—was it right that those distinguished citizens should have the property, and that nothing save the name should descend to Satrius? Forsooth, if he who does not, when he can, ward off or repel wrong is guilty of injustice (as I showed in the First Book), what is to be thought of him who, so far from repelling, abets the wrong? To me, indeed, genuine inheritances do not seem right, if sought by knavish blandishments,—by attentions rendered not from sincere but simulated kindness.[4] In such affairs, one thing sometimes appears expedient, another right. But it is a deceptive appearance; for the standard of expediency is the same as that of right. He who does not clearly see this is capable of any kind of fraud, of any crime. For he who thinks, "That is indeed right, but this is expedient," will dare in his ignorance to divorce things united by nature,—a state of feeling which is the source of all frauds, wrongs, crimes.

19. Therefore, if a good man could by snapping his fingers make his name creep surreptitiously into rich men's wills, he would not use this power, no, not even though he were absolutely certain that no one would ever have the least suspicion of it. But had you given this power to Marcus Crassus, that by snapping his fingers he could get his name inserted in a will though he were not really the heir, I warrant

---

1. Hortensius. As rival orators, cicero and Hortensius might have been on other than friendly terms, had they not both been intimate friends of Atticus.

2. Cicero charged Crassus with complicity in Catiline's conspiracy, and Crassus was a friend of Clodius, Cicero's bitterest enemy. After Cicero's return from exile, Crassus sought a formal reconciliation with Cicero, and there was no subsequent manifestation of hostility on his part.

3. It was shameful, as Cicero could not but think, that states whose citizens nominally enjoyed the rights of Roman citizenship should need official patrons, and equally so, in his esteem, that those patrons should be, like Satrius, selected from among Antony's adherents and satellites.

4. It is a singular feature of Roman society in and after Cicero's time that the legacy-hunters (*heredipetae*) should have been numerous enough and should have found dupes enough to form a distinct class, and almost a recognized profession.

you he would have danced in the forum. A just man, however, and one whom we feel to be a good man, will take nothing from any one to transfer it to himself. Let him who marvels at this confess that he knows not what a good man is. But if one would only develop the idea of a good man wrapped up in his own mind, he would then at once tell himself that he is a good man who benefits all that he can, and does harm to no one unless provoked by injury.[1] What then? Must not he do harm, who, as if by enchantment, displaces the true heirs, to put himself in their stead? "Is he not, then," some one may say, "to do what is serviceable, what is expedient?" Yes, but let him understand that nothing unjust can be either expedient or serviceable. He who has not learned this cannot be a good man. In my boyhood I heard from my father that Fimbria, who had been consul, was appointed judge in the case of Marcus Lutatius Pinthias, a Roman knight, not otherwise than respectable, who had laid a wager, to be forfeited if he did not prove himself to be a good man. Fimbria said that he would never act as judge in the case, lest, if he decided against Pinthias, he might deprive a worthy man of his reputation, or if he decided in his favor, he might seem to have pronounced some ordinary person to be a good man, while such a character was made up of innumerable duties and merits. To a good man, then, even in the conception of Fimbria, not to say of Socrates,[2] nothing can by any possibility seem expedient that is not right. Therefore such a man will not dare, not only to do, but even to think anything which he may not venture to proclaim publicly. Is it not shameful that philosophers should be in doubt about these matters as to which even peasants have no doubt? From the peasants sprang the old saying that has become proverbial. When they commend any one's honesty and goodness, they say that you might trust him to play odd and even[3] with you in the dark. What does this mean, unless that what

---

1. See Book I. § 7.

2. Of a man of the world, not of a philosopher.

3. Latin, *mices. Micare*, or *micare digitis* (to flash with the fingers), denotes the game of *mora*, which is still a favorite recreation, or rather mode of gambling, with the Roman populace, and may be often seen in the streets. Story, in his *Roba di Roma*, describes it as follows: "Two persons place themselves opposite each other, holding their right hands closed before them. They then simultaneously and with a sudden gesture throw out their hands, some of the fingers being extended, and others shut up on the palm,—each calling out in a loud voice, at the same moment, the number he guesses the fingers extended by himself and his adversary to make. If neither cry out aright, or if both cry out aright, nothing is gained or lost; but if only one guess the true number, he wins a point."

is unbecoming is not expedient, even if you could obtain it without any one being able to prove it against you? Do you not see that according to this proverb there could be no apology either for that Gyges of whom I have spoken, or for this man whom I just now supposed by way of illustration, who by snapping his fingers could convert the inheritances of a whole community to his own use? For as what is immoral, though concealed, cannot be in any way made right, so it cannot be brought about that, in spite of the opposition and repugnancy of nature, what is not right should in any case be expedient.

20. Yet it may be said that when the gain is very great, there is justifying cause for wrong-doing. When Caius Marius had no near prospect of the consulship, and still remained in obscurity the seventh year after he had been praetor, nor gave any token that he was ever going to offer himself as a candidate for the consulship, having been sent to Rome by his commander Quintus Metellus, a man and citizen of the highest eminence, whose lieutenant he was, he charged Metellus before the Roman people with needlessly protracting the war, intimating that if they had made him consul, he would in a short time have given Jugurtha either living or dead into the power of the Roman people. And so he was indeed made consul; but in bringing into odium by a false accusation a citizen of the highest worth and eminence, whose lieutenant he was[1] and by whom he had been sent home, he made a wide departure from good faith and honesty. My kinsman Gratidianus[2] did not play the part of a good man on the occasion when he was praetor, and the tribunes of the people had called into counsel the college of praetors, that the currency might have its standard fixed by a joint resolution; for the value of money was then so fluctuating that no one could know how much or how little property he had. The tribunes and praetors jointly framed a decree, specifying the penalty and the judicial proceedings for its violation, and agreed to mount the rostrum together in the afternoon. The others went their several ways; while Marius from the seats of the tribunes directly mounted the rostrum, and alone announced the decree which had resulted from their combined action. This affair, if you want to know, brought him

---

1. The relation of a *legatus*, or lieutenant, to his commander was, in Roman ethics, not unlike that of a son to his father, so that Marius in his conduct toward Metellus might have been pronounced *impius*.

2. Marcus *Marius* Gratidianus, son of an adopted son of the brother of Caius Marius.

great popularity. Statues were erected in his honor in all the streets; incense and wax tapers were burned before them. To cut the story short, no man was ever more cherished by the multitude. These are the cases which sometimes perplex one in the discussion,—cases where the matter in which honesty is transgressed is not so very great, while that which is obtained by means of it is of the very highest value; as, for Marius, it was not so irredeemably shameful to forestall the popular favor from his colleagues and the tribunes of the people, while by this means to become consul, the end which he then had in view,[1] seemed in the highest degree desirable. But there is one rule for all cases, which I would have profoundly impressed on your mind,—either that what seems expedient must not be wrong, or if it be wrong, that it must not seem to be expedient. Can we deem either that Marius or this a good man? Unfold and examine[2] your own consciousness, that you may see what within it is the aspect, shape, and conception of a good man. Does it fall in with the character of a good man to lie, to slander, to forestall, to deceive? Nothing certainly can be less in harmony with it. Is there, then, any object of so much value, or any advantage so worthy of your quest, that you should forfeit for it the glory and reputation of a good man? What is there that so-called expediency can bring to you of equal worth with what it takes from you, if it robs you of the reputation of a good man, and deprives you of truth and honesty? For what difference does it make, whether one turns himself from a man into a beast, or in the form of a man carries the moral obduracy of a beast?

21. What? Do not those who violate all that is right and virtuous if they can only obtain power, do the same thing with him who chose to have even for a father-in-law the man by whose audacity he himself might become powerful?[3] It seemed expedient to him to avail himself of the other's unpopularity for his own great advancement. He did not perceive how unjust this was to the country, how base, and how harmful. The father-in-law himself had always on his lips the Greek verses from the Phoenissae, which I will render as I can, awkwardly it may be, but still so as to be intelligible:—

---

1. He never obtained the consulship; but the very popularity won by his agency in settling the fluctuating currency was in Sulla's eyes a crime which made him one of the dictator's earliest victims.

2. Latin, *explica atque excute*, literally, unfold and shake out.

3. Pompey married Caesar's daughter, and hoped to gain ascendency by throwing upon Caesar the unpopularity of whatever was offensive in the measures of the triumvirate.

> "Transcend the right in quest of power alone;
> In all things else hold fast the bond of kindred."

It was criminal in Eteocles,[1] or rather in Euripides, to except that one thing which was the most wicked of all. Why, then, do we gather up crimes on a small scale, fraudulent heirships, bargains, sales? Here you have a man who desired to be king of the Roman people, and who accomplished his purpose. Whoever says that this desire was right, is mad; for he approves of the destruction of laws and of liberty, and deems their foul and detestable suppression glorious. But as for him who acknowledges that it is not right to usurp sovereign power in a state which was and which ought to be free, yet that it is expedient for him who can do so, by what remonstrance, or rather by what reproach, can I strive to draw him back from so grave an error? For (ye immortal gods!) can the basest and foulest parricide[2] committed upon his country be expedient for any man, even though he who has made himself thus guilty be called parent by the citizens whom he has brought under the yoke? Expediency, then, ought to be measured by the right, and so indeed, that the two, though expressed by different names, may have to the ear the same sound. I do not accord with the opinion of the multitude who ask what can be more expedient than the possession of sovereign power; on the other hand, I find nothing more inexpedient for him who has obtained this power unjustly, when I begin to recall reason to things as they really are. For can anxieties, solicitudes, terrors by day and by night, a life crowded full of snares and of perils, be expedient for any one? Attius says,

> "The throne has many faithless, loyal few."

But of what throne does he say this? Of one that was held by right, transmitted from Tantalus and Pelops. How much more, think you, must those words apply to that king who by the army of the Roman people subdued that very Roman people, and forced to servile obedience a state not only free, but ruling over whole races of men? What

---

1. Words put into the mouth of Eteocles when, having agreed to hold the sovereignty of Thebes with his brother on alternate years, he refused to resign the throne at the end of the first year.

2. The term parricide (*parricidium*) was always employed with reference to heinous crimes against the country (*patria*) as well as to the murder of a father.

misgivings of conscience must he have had on his mind, think you? What inward wounds? Whose life can be serviceable to himself if he holds it on condition that whoever deprives him of it will rise to the summit of favor and glory? But if these things which seem in the highest degree expedient are yet inexpedient because full of disgrace and wickedness, we ought to be thoroughly convinced that there is nothing expedient that is not right.

22. This, while often indeed at other times, was expressly decreed by Caius Fabricius in his second consulate and by our Senate, in the war with Pyrrhus. For Pyrrhus having made war with the Roman people without provocation, and there being a contest for supremacy with that high-minded and powerful king, a deserter came from him to the camp of Fabricius, and promised that, if he would give him his price, as he had come secretly, so he would return secretly to the camp of Pyrrhus, and kill him by poison. Fabricius sent the man back to Pyrrhus, and that act of his was commended by the Senate. Yet if we look to the appearance and the popular opinion of expediency, a single deserter would have put an end to that great war and to a dangerous enemy of the empire. But it would have been a great disgrace and scandal for one with whom the contest was for glory to have been overcome by crime, not by valor. Which, then, was the more expedient, for Fabricius, who was in this city what Aristides was in Athens, or for the Senate, which never divorced expediency from honor, to contend with the enemy by arms, or by poison? If empire is to be sought for the sake of glory, let crime, in which there can be no glory, be excluded; but if power be sought by any means whatsoever, it can be of no service conjoined with infamy. Therefore the proposal of Lucius Philippus, the son of Quintus, was not expedient, namely, that the states which by a decree of the Senate Lucius Sulla, for money received from them,[1] had freed from tribute should be taxed again, without our returning to them the money that they had paid for their exemption. The Senate assented to the proposal, to the disgrace of the empire. Pirates keep better faith. But it may be said that the revenues were increased, and it was therefore expedient. How long will men dare to call anything expedient that is not right? Can odium and infamy be of service to any empire, which

---

1. Probably some of the petty states that had been obtained by the conquest of Mithridates, and to which Sulla had sold this exemption for the money needed to pay his army.

ought to be supported by glory and by the good-will of its allies? I was often at variance even with my friend Cato. He seemed to me to guard the treasury and the revenues too obstinately, to refuse everything to the farmers of the revenue,[1] and many things to our allies; while we ought to be generous to our allies, and to deal with the farmers of the revenue as leniently as we individually do with our own tenants, especially as the union of orders[2] to which such a course would conduce is for the well-being of the state. Curio, too, was entirely in the wrong, when he said that the cause of the colonies north of the Po[3] was just, but always added, "Let expediency prevail." He should have said that it was not just because it was not expedient for the state, rather than have acknowledged it as just while saying that it was not expedient.

23. The Sixth Book of Hecato's treatise on Duties is full of such questions as these. "Ought a good man in a time of extreme dearth to continue to furnish food to his slaves?" He discusses both sides of the question, yet at the last makes expediency rather than humanity the standard of duty. He asks, "If in a storm at sea something must be thrown overboard, shall it be a valuable horse, or a slave of no value?" In this case interest inclines in one direction, humanity in the other. "If in case of shipwreck a fool gets possession of a plank, shall a wise man wrest it from him if he can?" He answers in the negative, because it would be unjust. "What may the master of the ship do in such a case? May he not take possession of the plank as his own property?" Not by any means. He has no more right to do this than to throw a passenger from the ship into the sea because the ship is his own. Until it arrives at the port to which passage has been taken, the ship belongs not to the master, but to the passengers. "What if there be but one plank for two shipwrecked passengers, both wise men? Shall they both try to get possession of it, or shall one yield to the other?" One should give it up to the other; but let that other be the one whose life is the more valuable, either for his own sake or for that of the state. "What if their claims are

---

1. They were sometimes in the position of rural tenants when the crops failed. There were times when the under-farmers (*portitores*) could not make their collections of taxes in full and in due season; but Cato was in favor of the most rigid treatment of the farmers-general (*publicani*), however they might fare with their subordinates.

2. The farmers of the revenue were of equestrian rank, and it was deemed desirable that the *equites* should be on good terms with the Senate.

3. They had claimed the full rights of citizenship in common with the colonies south of the Po,—a claim which Caesar granted.

equal?" There must be no quarrel between them, but one must yield to
the other, as if he had come off second-best in drawing lots or at odd
and even. "What if a father pillages temples, or makes an underground
passage to the public treasury? Shall the son give information to the
magistrates?" That indeed would be wrong. Nay, he may even defend
his father if he should be publicly accused. "Does not then duty to the
country take precedence of all other duties?" Yes, indeed; but it is for
the welfare of the country to have citizens dutiful toward their parents.
"What if the father should attempt to usurp supreme authority, or to
betray the country? Shall the son keep silence?" Yes, but he will implore
his father not to do so. If that is of no avail, he will take him earnestly
to task; will even threaten him; yet at the last, if there is danger of great
harm to the country, he will prefer the country's safety to his father's
safety. He asks also, "If a wise man by an oversight takes counterfeit
coins for good, when he ascertains what they are, shall he pay them
for good money to his creditors?" Diogenes says, Yes; Antipater, No,
and I agree with him. "Ought the seller of wine that he knows will not
keep, to tell his purchasers?" Diogenes says that there is no need of it;
Antipater thinks that a good man would tell. These questions are like
mooted points of law, among the Stoics. "In selling a slave, are his faults
to be told? Not such faults as, if not mentioned, would by the civil law
throw the slave back upon the vender's hands, but such as his being a
liar, a gambler, thievish, a drunkard?" Antipater says that they are to be
told; Diogenes, that they are not. "If any one selling gold thinks that it
is brass that he is selling, will a good man tell him that it is gold, or will
he buy for a shilling[1] what is worth a thousand shillings?" It is plain
enough by this time what I think of these things, and what a difference
of opinion there is among the philosophers that I have named.[2]

24. It is asked whether agreements and promises are always to be
kept, if made—to borrow the language of the praetorian edict—neither
by force nor by criminal fraud. If one had given to a person a remedy
for the dropsy, and had stipulated that he should never afterward use

---

1. Latin, *denarius.* The *denarius* was about equivalent to our New England shilling.
2. Though Cicero seems to have thought rightly on these questions, the very fact that
they could be mooted among members of the school of philosophy most noted for its high
ethical standard, gives us a not very favorable impression of pre-Christian ethics; and
the contrast between these Stoics and certain of the post-Christian, though non-Christian
moralists, gives color to the belief that Christianity had somehow penetrated where it
was not recognized.

the medicine,—in case that person, having been cured by the medicine, were to contract the same disease some years afterward, and could not obtain from him with whom he had made the agreement leave to use the remedy again, what ought he to do? Since he who would refuse such a request would be inhuman, and no harm can be done to him by using the remedy, regard should be paid to life and health. What, if a wise man were asked by one who wants to make him his heir to the amount of a million of sesterces,[1] to promise that before taking possession of his legacy he will dance in the forum publicly by daylight, and if without this promise the testator would not have given the legacy? Shall he keep his promise, or not? I should prefer that he had not made the promise, and this I think would have befitted his dignity. But since he has made the promise, if he thinks it disgraceful to dance in the forum, the least immoral falsehood of the two will be for him to break his promise and decline the legacy, unless, perchance, he can expend that money for the state in some great emergency of need, so that even dancing in the forum for the country's benefit would not be disgraceful.

25. Nor yet are those promises to be kept which are not for the advantage of those to whom you have made them. To go back to myths, Phoebus having promised his son Phaethon that he would do whatever he wished, the son wished to be taken up into his father's chariot. He was taken up, and before he was fairly seated, he was consumed by a thunderbolt. How much better would it have been if in this case the father's promise had not been kept! What shall be said of the promise that Theseus exacted of Neptune? Neptune having promised to grant him three wishes, he asked for the death of his son Hippolytus, whom he suspected of intrigue with his stepmother; but when Theseus had obtained his wish he was plunged into the deepest sorrow.[2] What shall we say of Agamemnon, who, having vowed to Diana the most beautiful creature that should be born that year in his kingdom, immolated Iphigenia, because no creature more beautiful was born that year in the kingdom? It would have been better not to keep the promise than to commit so foul a crime. Therefore promises are sometimes not to

---

1. Nearly half a million of our money.

2. In Book I. § 10, this example is used to substantially the same purpose,—the object there being to show, under the head of justice, that the literal keeping of a promise may, under some peculiar stress of circumstances, be virtually wrong; while here the proposition is that the intense stress of expediency may make that right which has the *prima facie* aspect of wrong.

be kept, nor are deposits always to be returned. If one had deposited a sword with you when he was of sound mind, and were to ask for it in a fit of insanity, to restore it would be wrong; not to restore it, your duty. What if he who had deposited money with you were to levy war against the country? Should you deliver up the trust? I think not; for you would act against the state, which ought to be nearest to your affection. Thus many things which seem to be right by nature become wrong by circumstances. To keep promises, to abide by agreements, to restore trusts, by a change of expediency becomes wrong. I think that I have now said all that is necessary about those things that seem to be expedient under the pretext of prudence, yet are really opposed to justice.

But since in the First Book I derived duties from four sources of right, I will adopt the same division in showing how hostile to virtue are those things that seem to be expedient, yet are not so. I have already, indeed, treated of prudence which cunning would fain imitate, and of justice which is always expedient. There remain two divisions of the right, one of which is witnessed in the greatness and superiority of a lofty mind; the other, in the shaping and government of the life by self-restraint and temperance.

26. It seemed expedient to Ulysses,[1]—as the story has come to us through some of the tragedians;[2] Homer throws no such suspicion on him, but there are tragedies that charge him with having purposed to escape service in the war by feigning insanity. The purpose was not right. "Yet it was expedient," some one perchance will say, "to reign in Ithaca, and to live at his ease with his parents, with his wife, with his son. Do you think any honor won in daily labors and perils to

---

1. I leave the ellipsis as it stands in the original.

2. Notably, Euripides and Sophocles, as also some of the Roman tragedians. The story is that he, as one of Helen's suitors, was the first to propose the oath by which they bound themselves, in case the marital rights of the successful suitor should be invaded, to join in defending or avenging him. But when he was called upon to fulfil his part of the covenant, he feigned insanity, yoked an ox and an ass together, ploughed a field with them, and sowed it with salt. Palamedes took Telemachus, and placed him where his father's plough would go over him, and Ulysses, by stopping his plough so as to avoid doing harm to the child, showed that he was not demented, and was thus compelled to keep his agreement and to bear his illustrious part in the Trojan war.

Palamedes, even a more decidedly mythical personage than Ulysses, is fabled to have been the inventor of light-houses, measures, scales, the discus, dice, the alphabet, and the mode of regulating sentries,—in fine, an impersonation of nearly all the practical wisdom of the old world.

be compared with this quiet life?" I, indeed, think that this quiet life
was to be despised and spurned; for the repose which was not right
I cannot regard as expedient. What, think you, would Ulysses have
heard, had he persevered in his pretended insanity? when, after his
greatest achievements in the war, he hears from Ajax:—

> *"He who first took the oath, and he alone,*
> *As you all know, forswore his plighted faith.*
> *Madness he feigned, the compact to evade,*
> *And had not Palamedes, with keen vision*
> *And wise device, unmasked his craft and cunning,*
> *He still had been a perjured recreant."*[1]

It was, indeed, better for him to fight, not only with the enemy, but
with the waves, as he did, than to desert Greece confederated with
one mind to carry war into the country of the barbarians.[2] But let us
leave myths and foreign instances. Let us come to fact and to our own
history. Marcus Atilius Regulus, when in his second consulship[3] he was
captured by troops in ambush under Xanthippus the Lacedaemonian,—
Hamilcar, Hannibal's father, being commander-in-chief,—was sent to
the Senate under oath that, unless certain prisoners of high rank were
restored to the Carthaginians, he would himself return to Carthage.
He on his arrival at Rome saw the semblance of expediency—but, as
fact shows, regarded it as delusive—to be in his own home, with his
wife, with his children; to maintain unimpaired his consular dignity,
regarding the calamity which he had incurred in battle as but a common
incident in the fortunes of war. Who can deny that this was expedient?
Who, think you? Magnanimity and Fortitude deny this.

27. Do you ask for better authorities? It is the property of these
virtues to fear nothing, to despise all human vicissitudes, to think
nothing that can happen to man intolerable. And so what did he do? He
came to the Senate; he stated his mission; he refused to give his own vote
in the case, because so long as he was bound by his oath to the enemy
he was not a senator. He, however, denied the expediency of sending
back the prisoners of war ("O foolish man," some one may have said,

---

1. These verses are from the *Armorum Judicium* of Pacuvius.
2. The Greeks called all except themselves barbarians.
3. He was proconsul in Africa, his second consulship having expired the previous
year.

"to contend against his own interest"); for the prisoners were young men and good leaders, while his vigor was already impaired by age. By virtue of his influence the prisoners were retained. He himself returned to Carthage, nor did his love for his country or his kindred retain him. Yet he then well knew that he was returning to an implacably cruel enemy and to excruciating punishment; but he considered his oath as binding. Thus when he was killed by being deprived of sleep[1] he was in a better condition than if he had remained at home, a captive old man, a perjurer of consular dignity. "Yet he acted foolishly, in not only declining to vote in favor of sending the prisoners back, but in also giving his advice against their release." How, foolishly? Did he act foolishly, if it was for the good of the state? Can what is harmful to the state be expedient for any citizen?

28. Men subvert the very foundations of nature when they separate expediency from the right. For we all seek what is expedient, and are drawn toward it, nor can we anyhow resist its attraction. Forsooth, who is there that shuns the things that are expedient? Or rather, who is there that does not pursue them with the utmost earnestness? But because we never can find what is expedient, save in good report, honor, right, we therefore esteem these first and highest; we regard expediency thus defined as not so much respectable as indispensable. "What is there in an oath?" some one may say. "Do we fear the anger of Jupiter? It is indeed an opinion common to all philosophers, not only to those who believe that the Deity neither does anything nor makes manifestation of himself to any other being,[2] but equally to those who suppose him always active in the government and direction of events,[3] that the Deity is never angry and never does harm. But what more harm could an angry Jupiter have done than Regulus did to himself? There was then no power of religion that could supersede expediency so weighty. Was his motive to avoid acting basely? In the first place, the least of evils

---

1. Accounts as to the death of Regulus vary,—some saying that he was put into a chest studded in the inside with nails; others, that his eyebrows were cut off, and his face then exposed to the full glare of an African sun; while it would seem that Cicero had a still different account, that he died from enforced wakefulness. Niebuhr sees no reason to suppose that he was tortured or killed, indeed, has very little faith in any part of his story, and it is maintained by some of the writers of his school that the report of his being so tortured was circulated in Rome to excuse the cruelties perpetrated by the family of Regulus on Carthaginian captives committed to their charge.

2. The Epicureans.

3. The Stoics.

are to be chosen. Was then the evil in the baseness of which you speak so great as that of the torture which he had to bear? Then again, this sentiment from Attius,—

> 'Faith hast thou broken?'
> 'I neither gave nor give faith to the faithless,'[1]

although put into the mouth of an impious king, yet is admirably well said." They add also that as we say that some things seem expedient that are not so, in like manner they say that some things seem right that are not so,—as, for instance, this very thing, returning to torture for the sake of preserving an oath inviolate seems right, yet becomes wrong, because a promise extorted by force ought not to be ratified. They still further say that whatever is highly expedient becomes right, even if it did not seem so before.

29. This is the substance of the case against Regulus. Let us now examine the first count. "He had no need to fear any harm from Jupiter's anger; for Jupiter is not wont either to be angry or to do harm." This argument is of no more force against Regulus than against any oath. But in an oath the point to be considered is not what it threatens, but what it means. For an oath is a religious affirmation. Therefore what you positively promise as in the presence of God ought to be performed. The question, then, no longer concerns the anger of the gods (for there is no such thing), but it is a question of honesty and good faith. Ennius well says:—

> "Oh genial, bright-winged Faith, and oath of Jove!"

He, then, who profanes an oath, profanes Faith, whom—as it is said in Cato's speech—our ancestors chose to have in the Capitol,[2] hard by the shrine of Jupiter Best and Greatest. "Then, too, Jupiter, if he had been angry, could not have done more harm to Regulus than Regulus did to himself." Undoubtedly, if pain were the only evil. But philosophers of the highest authority affirm, not only that pain is not the greatest evil, but that it is not even an evil. For the truth of this do not, I beg you, cast reproach on the testimony of Regulus, a witness not of moderate, but, so

---

1. This is from the *Atreus* of Attius. Thyestes asks Atreus, *Fregistin fidem?* and Atreus replies that he denies the obligation of keeping good faith with treacherous men.

2. Numa was said to have built a temple to Fides on the Capitoline Hill.

far as I know, of the very highest credibility; for what more trustworthy
witness can you ask than the chief man of the Roman people, who of his
own accord endured torture that he might keep duty inviolate? Then,
as to what they say about "the least of evils,"—namely, that meanness
is to be preferred to calamity,—is there any evil greater than meanness?
If such meanness as there is in the case of bodily deformity has in it
something offensive, in what vile esteem ought the depravation and
foulness of soul to be held! Therefore those who take the strongest
ground on these matters dare to affirm that meanness of soul is the
only evil; those who speak with more laxity do not hesitate to call it
the greatest of evils. As to the saying,

> *"I neither gave nor give faith to the faithless,"*

the poet had a right to say this; for in bringing Atreus upon the stage,
he had to support the character. But if those who are reasoning against
Regulus assume that the faith pledged to a faithless person is null, let
them look to it lest there be found here a subterfuge for perjury. Even
belligerents have rights, and an oath is often to be kept sacred with an
enemy. For what was so sworn that the mind of him who took the oath
at the time confessed the obligation, ought to be fulfilled; what was not
so sworn may be left unfulfilled without perjury.[1] Thus you would not
pay robbers a price that you had agreed to pay for your life; it is no
wrong if you fail to do this after having promised with an oath. For a
robber[2] is not included in the list of belligerents, but is the common
enemy of all. Between him and other men there ought to be neither
mutual confidence nor binding oath. For it is not simply swearing what
is false that constitutes perjury; but it is perjury not to perform what
you have sworn, as it is expressed in our legal form, in the purpose of
your own mind. Euripides makes a proper distinction when he says:—

> *"I swore in words; my mind I keep unsworn."*[3]

---

1. The most patent sophistry. If the sincerity with which an oath is taken be the
sole ground of its sacredness, free license is opened for unnumbered forms of perjury,—
certainly for the proverbially untrustworthy custom-house oaths, than which the civiliza-
tion of our time has had no fouler opprobrium.

2. Latin, *pirata*, which commonly means a robber by sea, yet is sometimes used, as
here, in the same sense with *praedo*, a robber by land.

3. From the Hippolytus. Unfortunately for Cicero's use of these words, which Euripides puts into the mouth of Hippolytus, the oath is regarded as sacred. He had sworn

But Regulus was bound in duty not to violate conditions and agreements made in war and with an enemy; for his concern was with a rightful and legitimate enemy, and as to such enemies our whole fecial law and many mutual rights were valid between them and us. If it were not so, the Senate would never have surrendered to enemies men of renown as prisoners.

30. This they did in the case of Titus Veturius and Spurius Postumius, who, in their second consulship, after the defeat at Caudium when our soldiers passed under the yoke, having concluded a peace with the Samnites without the consent of the people and the Senate,[1] were delivered up to the Samnites. At the same time Tiberius Numicius and Quintus Maelius, then tribunes of the people, because the peace had been concluded by their authority, were also surrendered, to consummate the repudiation of the treaty with the Samnites. Moreover, Postumius himself, who was among those surrendered, advised and supported the measure. Many years afterward the same thing was done by Caius Mancinus, who, having made a treaty with the Numantians without authority from the Senate, was surrendered to them, he himself advising the passage by the people of the decree to that effect, reported from the Senate by Publius Furius and Sextus Atilius. He acted more honorably than Quintus Pompeius, who when he was in the same case begged to be let off, and the decree of surrender was not passed. Here what seemed expedient preponderated over the right; in the former instances the false show of expediency was outweighed by the authority of the right. "But a promise exacted by force ought not to be performed." As if force could be brought to bear upon a brave man. "Still, why did he go to the Senate for the special purpose of dissuading them from surrendering the prisoners?" In asking this question, you cast reproach on what was greatest in Regulus. For he did not make himself judge in his own case; he undertook the management of the case that the Senate might decide upon it, and unless he had led the way to the decision by

---

that he would not divulge Phaedra's guilty secret to his father, and in the scene from which this verse is taken he says that but for the oath into which he had been entrapped unawares, nothing could have prevented him from telling his father the whole truth.

1. The commanders, even were they the consuls, could not lawfully make a treaty. The most that they had a right to do was to make a truce or an armistice, or to name terms of peace to be ratified by the Senate and people. The principle thus recognized is so obvious that if war be not, in Cicero's phrase, "opposed to nature," it might seem to belong to the law of nature no less than to the law of nations.

his authority, the prisoners would have been returned. Thus Regulus would have remained safe in his own country. Because he thought that this was not expedient for the country, he believed it right for himself to express his opinion and to suffer. Still further, as to their saying that whatever is highly expedient becomes right, the truth is that it is right, not that it becomes right. For nothing is expedient which is not also right, nor is anything right because it is expedient, but expedient because it is right. Therefore from many remarkable examples it would be difficult to name one more praiseworthy or illustrious than this.

31. Of all that is thus praiseworthy in the conduct of Regulus the one thing specially worthy of admiration is that he gave his advice in favor of retaining the prisoners. That, having thus advised, he returned, now seems to us admirable; in those times he could not have done otherwise. This merit therefore belongs to the times, not to the man; for our ancestors considered no bond more stringent than an oath in securing good faith. This is declared by the Sacred Laws;[1] it is declared by treaties in which good faith even with an enemy is made binding; it is declared by the examinations and sentences of the censors, who used to take no more diligent cognizance of any other subject than they took of oaths. Marcus Pomponius, tribune of the people, gave notice of an impeachment to Lucius Manlius, son of Aulus, after his dictatorship, because he had illegally added a few days to the term of his dictatorship. He also reproached him with having banished his son Titus from society and ordered him to live in the country. When the young man, the son of Manlius, heard that legal proceedings were instituted against his father, he is said to have hastened to Rome, and to have come to the house of Pomponius at early dawn. On his being announced, Pomponius, supposing that he had come in anger to bring some charge against his father, rose from his bed, and suffering none others to be present, gave orders for the young man to come to him. He, on entering, at once drew his sword, and swore that he would kill

---

1. Latin, *leges sacratae*. They were, probably, laws for the violation of which the criminal and his property were nominally consecrated to some god, i.e., he execrated and his property confiscated,—laws which had in Cicero's time become obsolete, as had the strict exercise of the censorial animadversion in the case of perjury. Of this class were the laws passed on Mons Sacer on the occasion of the first secession of the plebeians from Rome. Some commentators say that these laws were the only ones known as *leges sacratae*. Yet another opinion is that the *leges sacratae* corresponded to the canon law of Christendom,—that there were certain offences, perjury among the nest, the legal eognizance of which belonged to the priests.

Pomponius instantly unless he gave his oath to drop the prosecution. Pomponius, constrained by imminent peril, took the oath; did not lay the accusation before the people; told why he had been compelled to drop the case; discharged Manlius. Such was the importance attached to an oath in those times. This Titus Manlius is the one who obtained his surname[1] near the Anio from a collar taken from a Gaul who had challenged him and was killed by him, in whose third consulship the Latin army was scattered and put to flight near the Veseris,—a very distinguished man, as bitterly severe toward his son[2] as he had been excessively kind to his father.

32. But as Regulus merits renown for keeping his oath inviolate, so are those ten whom, after the battle of Cannae, Hannibal sent to the Senate under oath that they would return to the camp that had fallen into the possession of the Carthaginians, unless they obtained the redemption of the prisoners of war, to be held in the vilest esteem, if they really did not return. As to these men accounts vary.[3] Polybius, a fully trustworthy authority, says that of ten men of the highest rank who were sent, nine returned, not having obtained from the Senate the release of the prisoners, but that one who had gone back to the camp shortly after leaving it on the pretence of having forgotten something, remained in Rome. By his return to the camp he maintained that he was acquitted of his oath; but wrongly, for deceit aggravates perjury instead of annulling it. This was, then, a foolish cunning perversely assuming the aspect of prudence. The Senate, therefore, decreed that

---

1. Torquatus.

2. Shortly before this very battle of Veseris the consuls gave orders that no Roman should engage in single combat with any soldier of the opposing army. The son of Torquatus, driven almost to madness by the taunts and insults of a Tuscan soldier, accepted his challenge, killed him, and brought the trophies of the successful conflict to his father, who immediately ordered the youth to be beheaded.

3. This story, it will be remembered, is told in a slightly different form in Book I. § 13. The passage in which that version of it occurs is wanting in some manuscripts, and omitted in some editions; but the critical evidence is in its favor. It is appropriately told in each connection, and Cicero is never unwilling to tell the same story twice, if it will in each instance serve the purpose in hand. There seems to have been about the Punic wars, as about many passages of Roman history, a strange mingling of authentic narrative and popular tradition, so that of events that undoubtedly took place there are often several versions. The science of historical criticism had not been even conceived of, and we find that writers, Plutarch included, always select the version of a story that will best point a moral or illustrate a character. Aulus Gellius says that of the ten Romans sent home by Hannibal eight returned, and two who had evaded their oath by fraud remained in Rome, branded with ignominy by the censors, and the objects of universal contempt and scorn.

the rogue and cheat should be sent in chains to Hannibal. But there was something still greater on the part of the Roman people. Hannibal held as prisoners eight thousand men, who had not been taken in battle or escaped when in peril of death, but who had been left in camp by Paulus and Varro. The Senate refused to have them redeemed, though it might have been done for a small sum of money, that it might be ingrafted in the minds of our soldiers that they must either conquer or die. Polybius writes that when Hannibal heard this his spirit was broken, because the Senate and the Roman people had borne their reverses with so lofty a mind. Thus does what seems expedient sink out of account when brought into comparison with the right. I ought to add that Acilius, who wrote a history in Greek, says that there were several who returned to the camp to free themselves from their oath by the same equivocation, and that they were branded with every token of ignominy by the censors. We may close this head; for it is perfectly clear that whatever is done with a timid, sordid, abject mind—such as the action of Regulus would have been, had he either given his opinion concerning the prisoners in his own interest and not in that of the state, or consented to remain at home—is not expedient, because it is infamous, foul, base.

33. There remains the fourth division, comprehending becomingness, moderation, discretion, self-restraint, temperance. Can anything be expedient which is opposed to this choir[1] of such virtues? However, those of the Cyrenaic school[2] and the disciples of Anniceris,[3] philosophers only in name, followed Aristippus in making all good to consist in pleasure, and regarded virtue as commendable only in its pleasure-giving capacity. They having passed almost out of notice, Epicurus holds his ground as an advocate and teacher of nearly the same doctrine. With these I must contend, as the phrase is, with infantry and cavalry,[4] if

---

1. This figure is used in another instance by Cicero, in the *Tusculanae Disputationes*, Book V. It is also used once in the New Testament, where our English version gives no intimation of it, in 2 Peter i. 5. "With all diligence bring up and lead on in the choir [or dance] (ἐπιχορηγήσατε) on [or next to] faith, virtue," &c.

2. The Cyrenaic school was founded by Aristippus. See Book I. § 41, note.

3. Anniceris is regarded as having been of the Cyrenaic school, and differed from Aristippus chiefly in admitting that the social virtues are good in themselves, yet good because, though they sometimes give trouble, their pleasure-yielding capacity transcends the labor, inconvenience, and sorrow that may incidentally result from them.

4. Latin, *viris equisque*, literally, with men and horses, i.e., in full military array, with all the strength that I can muster, with might and main.

I mean to guard and maintain the right. For if not only expediency but everything appertaining to a happy life consists in a strong constitution of body and in a reasonable expectation of preserving that constitution, as Metrodorus[1] writes, certainly this expediency—the highest expediency in the opinion of those who thus reason—will be in conflict with the right. For where, in the first place, shall room be found for prudence? In raking together from every quarter objects to delight the senses? How wretched this slavery of virtue in bondage to pleasure! What, then, is the function of prudence? To choose pleasures intelligently? Grant that nothing can be more delightful than this, what can be imagined meaner? Then, again, what room is there for fortitude, which is the contempt of pain and labor, with him who calls pain the greatest of evils? For although Epicurus may in many places, as he does, speak bravely enough about pain, we are to look, not at what he says, but at what it is consistent for him to say, who acknowledged no good except pleasure, no evil except pain. Thus also, if I listen to him about self-restraint and temperance, he says indeed much in many places; but, as the phrase is, the water does not run.[2] For how can he commend temperance, who places the greatest good in pleasure? Temperance is inimical to the sensual appetites; but those appetites are the handmaids of pleasure. Yet as to these three virtues they shift and turn as they can, and with no little ingenuity. They bring in prudence as knowledge employed to supply pleasures, to drive away pain. They also explain fortitude after some fashion, calling it the method of taking no account of death and putting up with pain. Temperance, too, they drag in, not very easily indeed, but as well as they can, saying that the highest pleasure amounts to no more than the absence of pain. Justice totters, or rather lies prostrate, and so do all those virtues which belong to social life and the fellowship of the human race. Nor can there be goodness, or generosity, or courtesy, any more than friendship, if they are not to be sought on their own account, but only with reference

---

1. The disciple, inseparable companion, and intimate friend of Epicurus, and his destined successor, though Epicurus outlived him by seven years. He gave his master's philosophy its fullest development in the direction of sensuality, expressly and seriously maintaining that the organs of digestion furnish the true test and measure for everything appertaining to a happy life.

2. A figure derived from a watercourse whose flow is obstructed. The idea is: What he says about these virtues does not flow easily, as if he were sincere and thoroughly in earnest.

to pleasure. To sum up the whole in brief, as I have maintained that there is no expediency which is opposed to the right, so I affirm that all sensual pleasure is opposed to the right. All the more do I find fault with Calliphon and Dinomachus,[1] who thought that they were going to put an end to the controversy by uniting pleasure with the right, as they might yoke a beast with a man. The right does not accept this union, spurns it, repels it. Nor can the supreme good, which ought to be simple, be mingled and compounded of widely unlike ingredients. But of this—for it is a great theme—I treat more at length elsewhere.[2] As to the subject now in hand, I have sufficiently shown how the matter is to be decided, if at any time what seems to be expedient is repugnant to the right. But if sensual pleasure shall be said even to have the appearance of expediency, it cannot have any union with the right. To make such concession as we can in favor of pleasure, the most that we can say of it is that it may perhaps give some seasoning to life; it certainly is of no benefit.

You have from your father, my son Marcus, a gift, in my opinion, great; but that will be according to the use that you make of it. Although you are to take in these three books as guests among the lectures of Cratippus, yet as if, in case I had come to Athens—which I should indeed have done had not the country with a loud voice recalled me midway—you would sometimes have listened to me as well as to Cratippus—you would sometimes have listened to me as well as to Cratippus, so since my voice reaches you by means of these volumes, you will give them as much time as you can, and you can give them as much time as you please. When I shall have become fully aware that you take pleasure in science of this type, while I shall, as I hope, at no great distance of time, talk with you face to face, I shall none the less, while we are apart, converse with you though absent from you. Farewell, then, my Cicero, and believe that you are very dear to me, and will be much more dear if you shall find your happiness in writings like these and in such precepts as they contain.

---

1. Their doctrine was that for man pleasure and virtue are both ends of being,— pleasure by nature and from the beginning, virtue after experience of the good that there is in it.

2. In the Second Book of *De Finibus Bonorum et Malorum*.

www.ingramcontent.com/pod-product-compliance
Lightning Source LLC
Chambersburg PA
CBHW030526100426
42813CB00001B/168